FORWARD

At one point I collated everything I knew about story structure and drew a picture with it.

This book and its associated workbooks expand on that picture.

CHARACTER & STRUCTURE

AN UNHOLY ALLIANCE

CHRIS ANDREWS

CREATIVE MANUSCRIPT SERVICES

For my parents who told me I could do anything.

CONTENTS

Contents

THANK YOU

Thank you to Les Petersen and Rob Porteous who gave me their honest advice on early drafts, and to Jo Clay who took an editing knife to my typos, mixed metaphors and poor word choices.

Additionally, thank you to everyone who supported me with friendship, encouragement and feedback.

This book is better thanks to you.

1

A TRIP TO THE MOVIES

A while back I saw a movie trailer. I wasn't paying all that much attention, but the trailer looked like my sort of thing: a supernatural action flick.

I should have paid more attention.

My expectations took a huge hit when I discovered the cinema was full of teenage girls (and the occasional boyfriend who'd clearly been dragged along). The cinema was packed.

I felt myself sinking lower and lower into my seat. There might have been a couple of dads and mums taking their tween daughters, but they were harder to spot than Wally.

When the movie started, girls screamed. Literally. They screamed again when some of the characters made appearances. It was as if I'd I travelled to the sixties and Beatle-mania had taken hold.

Only it was a movie, not a band, and the movie was Twilight. I'd thought I was in for something similar to Underworld starring Kate Beckinsale. Not so much.

And yet... it's the story that changed my perspective on what stories need to do.

The movie had such a strong emotional grip on its audience that even though it could have used millions more to smooth out the rough edges, it both met and exceeded expectations and went on to spawn four sequels based on the follow-up books.

How did a story written for a very specific *romance sub-genre* sell hundreds of millions of copies and make a fortune at the box office?

Despite all the criticisms, Stephanie Meyer did something right when she wrote Twilight.

There were many other books that were big at the same time: The Girl with the Dragon Tattoo, the Harry Potter series, and the Hunger Games series to name just three. They all became very successful movies.

Something about those stories did more than just entertain. They reached *well beyond their genres* and became mainstream.

The Marvel Cinematic Universe has achieved the same thing, and if you care to look closely enough you'll realise it's because of the characters, not the world-building or cool superpowers.

Marvel took a huge risk and started out with characters many people had probably never heard of, such as Iron Man, Dr Strange and the Guardians of the Galaxy. They worked because Marvel put the characters first, and the audience engaged with these characters.

Stories are about people, not events. Structure is how you tailor events so your audience can engage with your characters.

You can do it too

We don't all have Disney backing our stories, but we do have access to the same techniques the Marvel Cinematic Universe uses.

The answers are in every successful story you've ever read or seen or heard.

All you need to do is ask the simplest question you can ask about a story. Why will anyone care? Delivering on that question requires story mastery.

So how do you make your audience care about your characters and what happens to them?

Hold your story up against that question and answer the questions in this book honestly. They'll illuminate a path you may not have been aware of before.

The Care Factor

Not too long ago my youngest daughter came charging down the stairs like a nuclear storm intent on flattening everything before it. She burst into the family room, bouncing with excitement. "They're going to do it! Finally!" she said before charging back up the stairs, leaving me baffled.

Less than a minute later she came running back down. "Yes! They did it Dad! They really did it!" I didn't know if she was going to hug me or run me down in an attempt to find someone else to tell she was so excited.

"What are you talking about?"

"They finally kissed! It took four books! Four!"

With that she disappeared back up the stairs to keep reading, her excess energy no longer sufficient to keep her away from the story.

I'm still not sure what series of books she was talking about, but she was definitely invested in them.

Emotions are the crucial factor in any story. A kiss is just a kiss unless your audience cares about the characters involved.

Here's two tough questions:

1. There's lots of great stories out there - what makes yours stand out?
2. Why should anyone care? (They won't just because you do.)

They're tough questions, but they're questions you should ask yourself when planning, rewriting, editing or troubleshooting. They apply to fiction and non-fiction alike, and across story mediums.

Looking at any story from a sales and marketing perspective, why would a publishing company, movie studio or theatre company spend money to produce your story when it's competing against millions of others (as well as free funny cat videos)?

- What do you feel about your story?
- What are you trying to make other people feel?

You need an answer to both questions. If the answer to either question is 'not much' then your chances of success are about the same.

People don't buy stories because they're full of brilliant ideas, they're after an emotional experience. How are you going to engage emotions and make people care about your characters?

The cause and effect is simple; if your audience cares, they're more likely to tell their friends who may also care, and so on. That's true even with negative emotions like the fear generated by horror movies, or tragedies like The Boy in the Striped Pyjamas.

If you think that's not true, visit the textbook section in any library. When was the last time someone recommend a textbook because they enjoyed reading it so much? They're full of information and they have a purpose, but that purpose is rarely entertainment.

Studio executives gamble millions (and sometimes billions) of dollars on the movies they produce. Publishers gamble thousands. Theatre companies invest heavily before the first actor walks onstage.

They all have to be fairly certain they'll get a return on their investment, and that means relying on the audience to respond to what they buy.

What do you want the industry gatekeepers to feel when they read your manuscript? Excitement that they have another success in their hands?

Romance is built on emotion and that's why it's the biggest selling genre on the planet. It's also the most generic example of storytelling you can find. In almost every single romance, the characters:

- meet
- fall in love
- break up
- get back together.

Romance is highly repetitive in the sense that the same basic events play out over and over, yet the stories are all different, or at least different enough that romance lovers keep consuming them.

Romance is entirely about the characters and what readers experience - not the events.

Every romance lover knows how the story's going to end before they start it, meaning that how it plays out is far more important than what happens.

Give me the same thing, only different

That's actually a saying in Hollywood: *Give me the same thing, only different*. I doubt that surprises you.

Your audience thinks along the same terms. It's why stories have beginnings, middles and ends. It's also why we have genres and sub-genres. Stories are pretty much the same, only different.

Too different means failing to meet your audience's expectations, and failing means... failing.

Being original and meeting expectations is a fine line to walk. The trick is to pour creativity onto the well-defined scaffolding of story structure.

Putting it into practice

- How do you feel about your story?
- What are you trying to make other people feel?
- How are you going to engage your audience's emotions?
- How are you going to make your audience care about your characters?

2

STRUCTURE

Structure is a map for creating emotional impact through conflict, not a series of steps to cross off a checklist.

Many writers develop an intuitive sense for what works but don't necessarily understand how or why those things work. That makes it difficult to fix problems or repeat successes.

That's not a good way to build a career. The world is littered with one-hit wonders.

Writers and their audiences unconsciously understand how stories work thanks to a lifetime of:

- television
- movies
- plays
- books
- graphic novels
- listening to other people talk about stories.

Building a career in the story business means being able to explain what you're doing and why you're doing it. It means consciously making choices about those things with every story you write.

You gain mastery through learning and application, not guesswork.

To go from a consumer to a master storyteller means understanding an audience's expectations and working toward them.

Breaking it down

In pure story terms:

Story structure = character journey.

Creativity is where the fun comes into the writing process and makes your story unique, original, fresh and enjoyable, while still meeting audience expectations.

Intentionally breaking from expectations means spending story time educating your audience in the hope you can alter their expectations to meet your story.

It can work, but you better know what you're doing and have a solid reason to diverge. Even if you get it right there's a good chance it'll limit your audience.

Where do expectations start?

Expectations begin on first impression: title, cover art, blurb, tagline, and anything you say about it.

Beyond that, an audience expects common elements: a beginning, middle and end, and certain points within those parts. From there, stories diverge with the use of genres, tropes, characters, problems and issues.

Above all else, your goal is to get your audience to invest in your characters. Original ideas and high concepts are a fantastic addition to almost any story, but they won't sell without relatable characters on a story path people understand.

Structure is all about laying the foundations for your protagonist's journey – translating the story in your head into something an audience understands.

So let's break it down.

3

BUILDING THE FOUNDATIONS

One plot to rule them all

If your characters mostly hold hands and sing songs, you can't expect everyone to love your story (except perhaps your mother, and that's a maybe).

Stories need a plot, and there's really only one plot. Yes, just one. If you're disappointed by that, read on for suitable twists, turns, and even a complication or two.

Broken down, your 'one plot to rule them all' has two essential parts:

- A problem
- A resolution

It really is that simple.

If you're going to write a story it's essential to figure out what the problem is and how you're going to resolve it. The alternative is like meandering through a sewage treatment facility – absolutely fascinating if that's your thing but unlikely to thrill most people.

Ask any writer what their latest work-in-progress is about, and if you don't get a sense of a story problem in the first few seconds gently steer them towards it. If it turns out they don't have a story problem, or have too many story problems, give them a copy of this book. Or run away.

From the earliest stories represented by cave paintings to decades-spanning television shows, and even massive multi-player online games involving hundreds of thousands of active participants, there's always a central problem.

It could be:

- put dinner on the table or starve
- defeat the evil overlord
- win a lover
- stop the war
- be the first person to cross an ocean... or an ocean of stars.

While there's always a problem, that doesn't mean there has to be an antagonist, but antagonists are the most obvious focus for a story problem. They're also the easiest to implement as bad guys embody the story problem and audiences love seeing a well-crafted antagonist get their comeuppance – just ask Joffrey Baratheon.

A story problem is only half the story. The flip-side of a problem is its resolution. A story needs an ending worthy of the problem. That could be as simple as roast lamb on the dinner table for the kids, or as divisive as a beauty pageant where the protagonist must defeat the contestant with the sweetest smile and biggest claws.

Regardless of the details, if your story is written for an audience, it needs a problem that gets resolved to their satisfaction.

Compelling story power

You need more than action scenes, glorious sunsets and hot sex to make your story compelling. Your story also needs:

- a threat of consequences
- conflict generated by the problem and the threat.

The **story problem** is the main issue *your protagonist must deal* with over the course of the story.

The **story threat** is the consequence(s) *of your protagonist failing* to deal with the story problem.

Conflict arises because it's really difficult for *your protagonist* to resolve the story's problem and avoid the consequences.

As the subtle art of italics demonstrates, all three elements relate to your protagonist (and by default their support crew or ensemble cast). Without characters who care about something, the story problem carries no threat and little conflict.

Consider this. If a planet with billions of people vaporises in another universe, what difference will it make to your next door neighbour?

If your characters don't care, nobody will. Having a problem your protagonist cares about (a lot) resonates with audiences.

Unless your audience is restricted to you, get a problem that produces a threat and consequences your characters won't like.

Once you know your story's main problem and the conflict it generates, you have the dramatic core of your story.

Audiences like drama.

Fast and fun exercise

Pick some successful stories you're familiar with (from any medium - books, movies, plays, graphic novels, etc.).

Write down:

- each story's main problem

- why each problem generates natural conflict within the story.

Here's a list of stories you might like to try:

- Lord of the Rings
- Peter Pan
- Pride and Prejudice (and Zombies perhaps)
- Fahrenheit 451
- Gulliver's Travels
- The Wizard of Oz
- Seven Samurai
- Some Like it Hot

Add as many more as you like. It's a fun warm-up exercise. For example:

Lord of the Rings

Main problem: Sauron wants to rule the world and will destroy anyone who stands in his way.

Conflict: Everything most people consider to be 'good' in the world will be destroyed, and they're not willing to accept that.

Your story's heart

Your story problem is your story's heart.

What kind of beast does it fit? A cricket? A dog? Perhaps an elephant or a giraffe? A Klingon? Like stories, they all have roughly the same parts, expressed differently.

If it's a beast nobody understands, like an alien that's so inhuman it's nearly incomprehensible, you've got a lot of explaining to do. Explaining takes time, usually gets boring, and reduces story engagement. Nothing's happening while you explain.

There are ways around it to some degree, so if you can disguise it well enough, go for it.

Conversely, something familiar to an audience takes no time. For example:

- A horse. (Are you imagining a horse now?)
- Alternatively: Something with rock-like skin from another universe that looks a bit green and tree-like, but we've never encountered it and can't readily describe it, or it's entirely inhuman motivations. Feel free to spend the next couple of chapters filling in the blanks about your alien. While you do that, my horse is trampling a young princess who fell from its back after the horse saw a snake, and the Kingdom is in chaos because it was the evil brother who dropped the snake and has plans to bump off his father and take the throne and rule the world...

Giving your audience something familiar means saving yourself a considerable amount of time and angst explaining it, convincing your audience to run with it, and revisiting your concept multiple times before it really sinks in.

Similarly, structure requires no effort (just understanding on your part).

That doesn't mean that using a standard story structure is the best option for every story, but it's certainly the easiest way to begin engaging an audience.

Familiar doesn't mean 'the same'. If a thousand people each paint a horse you'll have a thousand different horses (and maybe a couple of elephants or goats from the people that didn't understand the instructions), but most will be recognisable as horses.

Even a toddler can paint a horse, but only you can paint yours.

Taking it further

It's time to look at your story as a whole.

Imagine you're looking down on your story world right now and you're about to play the part of the Norse God Loki.

He's neither evil nor good. He's a trickster and mischief maker, but he makes life interesting.

You're Loki and you've got a perfectly good world spreading out before you. Perfect is boring, and being Loki the mischief maker you feel an unquenchable urge to stir up trouble.

As Loki, you need to threaten the characters with something like: an invading army, a rival for a pair of lovers, the shortage of essential medicines to save lives, etc.

It could be as simple as two lovers failing to get together and consequently losing their happily ever after, or as epic as the destruction of the universe.

Enjoy being Loki!

Examples of problems (Loki's perspective)

In Finding Nemo, Marlin and Coral are about to become parents. Everything's wonderful. If you were Loki and this was your story world, what would you do? If nothing had changed, Marlin and Coral would have lived happily ever after, raising kids and becoming grandparents. Boring! Unfortunately for Marlin, events take a devastating turn: Coral gets killed and all but one of their eggs are lost, leading to the story's main problem – an overprotective father. This results in Nemo rebelling and getting fish-napped.

What about a story like Star Wars, the most successful epic fantasy to ever dress up in Sci-fi drag? Imagine a perfect galaxy where benevolent Jedi help guide everyone toward enlightened lives and there's no dark side to the Force. Snooze-worthy for anyone but a studious monk on a learning bender. What would Loki do if given the reins to such a story world? Perhaps he'd throw in an evil empire and a planet-destroying Death Star, and a dark side to the Force? Without a little Loki interference there'd have been no stolen Death Star plans to shatter Luke's life, and Luke would have had no reason to go on an adventure.

Would The Matrix have been a success if the machines had no consciousness? What problem did the machines pose? What did the Gods of that story universe (the Wachowskis) do? They enslaved humanity by trapping them in a machine-controlled virtual reality world with nothing but the illusion of free will.

Imagine a high school. Any high school. A wonderful centre for learning and development where the teachers are brilliant and every student graduates with amazing grades and a pat on the back. What would Loki do if he wanted to cause a problem in such a perfect school? Maybe he'd turn it into a regular high school where a bright but bored kid wanted a day off. Perhaps Loki would give that school a kid like Ferris Bueller, as well as an anal Principal with an overinflated sense of duty. Such a Loki may even give Ferris a sister with a grudge. Without anyone else determined to catch him, Ferris could have taken the day off without any problems, but where'd be the fun in that?

What about something like the epic masterpiece Dune? In Dune, whoever controls the spice Melange controls the galaxy. What would happen if whoever controlled the spice shared it around evenly and everyone was happy with this? No story, right? Frank Herbert threw a little Loki mischief into the mix. The ruling Emperor practiced politics instead of benevolence, and pitted Houses against each other to stop them plotting against him. When Paul Atreides loses everything due to this infighting he goes after the only thing that matters - control of the spice Melange.

Where would a murder mystery be without a murder?

How many people would you interest if you wrote a romance that ran smoothly?

Where does that leave you as the Story God of Mischief? It means you need to create problems - one big one at least, and it has to be a problem your protagonist resolves by the end of the story.

Putting it into practice

As you go through this book, make sure you answer the questions and write your answers down somewhere.

If you haven't already done so, write down:

- your story's main problem
- what your *protagonist* needs to do to satisfactorily resolve the problem
- the consequences of failing to resolve the problem for:
- your protagonist
- the larger story world.
- what your *antagonist* (assuming you have one) needs to do to resolve the same problem and achieve *their* best outcome.
- what the results would be if your antagonist succeeds? Write answers for:
- your antagonist
- the larger story world
- how you're going to resolve the story problem.

4

THE THREAT

Your story's threat is the flip-side of your story's problem, the unrealised (and most likely, devastating) consequences that will happen if your protagonist fails to resolve the problem.

Take Avengers Infinity War, Part 1.

- The main story problem: Thanos is collecting the infinity stones so he can use them to wipe out half of all life in the galaxy.
- The threat: everyone will lose people they care about and/or their own lives.

Together, the problem and threat create a cause and effect scenario.

The threat in any story is the *potential* for anything your protagonist cannot and will not accept. The keyword is *potential*. It's also the main motivation for your protagonist.

As your audience generally sides with the protagonist there's only one real outcome you can offer them, but for the sake of drama you must make it look like the chances of failure are real.

In Star Wars (Episode IV), the story's threat was aptly demonstrated when the Death Star destroyed Alderaan. If it could destroy one world, it could destroy many more. The threat wasn't just the destructive potential of the Death Star, but what it meant for the galaxy.

It doesn't have to be galaxy-wide. The threat of losing your job or failing to make the football team can be just as devastating. The more emotionally devastating, the better.

Threat and emotional impact

To build the necessary emotional impact, the threat needs to have personal consequences for your protagonist and as many of the other main characters as possible. Who or what is threatened by the problem? Family? Friends? A kid's playground? A town or village or city? A world?

Why does your protagonist care? Will ignoring the story problem:

- Allow more guns onto the streets and into the hands of kids or criminals?
- Force the closure of a soup kitchen which feeds the homeless?
- Destroy a relationship?

Whatever the threat is, make it something your characters desperately care about. If they don't care, your audience won't care either.

Putting it into practice

In your story, what are the consequences of failure?

Write them down for:

- the protagonist
- the antagonist

- other characters as necessary

Additionally:

- Why does your protagonist care?
- Why does your antagonist care?
- Why do each of your other main characters care?

5

GENERATING NATURAL CONFLICT

As stated, there are three elements that combine to produce natural conflict within your story. They are:

- a significant problem
- the threat of undesirable consequences
- your protagonist's care factor (conflict).

You need a solid understanding of these elements to make conflict work on a character level.

Conflict is divided into three areas:

- **Internal** - such as, fear, doubt, and personal hang-ups.
- **External** - what the world throws at your characters, such as a war zone, adverse weather or natural disasters, or even a flat tyre when someone desperately needs to get somewhere.
- **Interpersonal** - problems between characters, such as overbearing shoulder-chips that rub other characters the wrong way, differences in perspective or needs when confronted with a shared issue, or simply from growing up in

opposing cultures or from differences in morals. Any issues that set people at odds with each other.

Each of these areas of conflict can appear at any level of your story, such as a single scene, a chapter, a story arc or the overall story. They can come and go at different times in a story, or act as the overall driver.

However you apply conflict, make sure it's absolutely essential to the story and what the characters care about.

If it's unrelated to the story and the story's main problem, it's irrelevant.

More importantly, if the characters don't care about it, there's no conflict.

Dramatic foundations

Every story, at least with regard to what's commonly perceived as a standard story structure in western cultures, follows the same basic pattern.

It's the telling of the tale that makes the difference between awesome and 'meh'. For a story to work, you need *drama*.

Drama evolves from a combination of:

- character
- problem
- threat.

Conflict is built on the *problems* your *characters* face, the *threat* of failure, and how much they care about the consequences. Conflict creates drama.

Generally speaking, the bigger the problem and the more significantly the consequences that may affect your characters, the stronger the story is likely to be.

It's a bit like math:

$$(Problem + Threat) \times Character\ Care\ Factor = Drama$$

This roughly translates into conflict, though there's a lot of influences, so consider it a starting point.

While nothing guarantees success, adding conflict is an essential part. Compelling conflict is the lifeblood of drama.

Putting it into practice

Whenever you think about any aspect of your story, whether a scene, a character, a plot point or twist, use it to make the most of conflict.

Not every scene demands conflict, but the few that don't should herald conflict. In this regard, think of an action movie where the good guys are 'suiting up'. There's not necessarily any conflict in the suit-up scene (seriously, they're just getting dressed), but the threat of conflict is present in the form of tension because they're heading toward conflict.

Take five minutes right now and brainstorm answers to these simple (but sometimes difficult to answer) questions.

What is *the main* source of conflict:

- in your story world (what's worth fighting for - resources, ideals, beliefs, power, control, freedom)?
- for your protagonist (why does it matter to them - why is it personal)?

How does this affect your protagonist:

- Internally?
- Externally?
- Through their relationships with other characters, both friends and foes?

Now, apply some additional questions to each of your answers.

- Why do you care as the writer?
- Why will an audience care?

This will give you some insight into why it's worth writing the story in the first place, both for you and your audience.

If you don't have any good answers for these questions, give it a few minutes and jot down whatever seems appropriate. You can change your answers later, but for now you need to find a place to work from.

Not having a clearly defined story problem, consequential threat and associated conflicts is a very easy mistake to make.

Don't make it.

Putting this section into practice should give you:

- The main source of conflict in your story world, why you care, and why an audience should care.
- Why this conflict is important for your protagonist, why it matters to you as well, and why your audience will empathise.

STORY STRUCTURE DIAGRAM
FANDELYON.COM

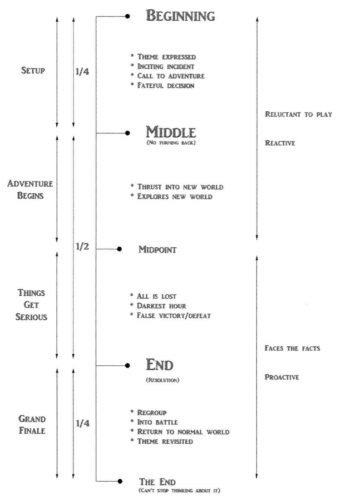

BEGINNING

* Theme expressed
* Inciting incident
* Call to adventure
* Fateful decision

Setup · 1/4

Reluctant to play

MIDDLE
(No turning back)

Reactive

Adventure Begins

* Thrust into new world
* Explores new world

1/2 · Midpoint

Things Get Serious

* All is lost
* Darkest hour
* False victory/defeat

Faces the facts

END
(Resolution)

Proactive

Grand Finale · 1/4

* Regroup
* Into battle
* Return to normal world
* Theme revisited

The End
(Can't stop thinking about it)

© Copyright Chris Andrews

6

HALVES

Now you've identified the story's problem, conflict and threat, how do you deliver them in a way your audience can appreciate on an emotional level?

Simple. You give them a narrative structure they're already familiar with; the good old beginning, middle and end, divided into halves.

Halves?

Take a look at the Story Structure Diagram. There's two clear halves. In terms of story, character journeys mirrors these two halves. The first half:

- sets up the problem and the conflicts your protagonist will face.
- asks questions your audience will want answered later in the story.

The second half:

- Escalates and resolves the conflict.

- Answers the questions you raise in the first half.
- Concludes the story in a way your audience will find satisfying.

That's your story's structure at its most basic level.

- First half = setup.
- Second half = resolution.

The set up and resolution must be delivered from your protagonist's perspective (or whatever character represents your theme if you've got an ensemble cast).

During the first half of the story your protagonist is learning about the story problem and how it affects them. They ask or face questions your audience would ask.

In the second half they take action to resolve the problem and find answers to their questions.

That doesn't necessarily mean you have to answer all the questions you raise, particularly if it's the first part of a longer series, but you have to tie up all essential questions related to the story's problem while promising answers in future instalments.

Think Game of Thrones. Winter is coming, but what does that mean? The fact that winter is coming isn't a story problem in the first book of the series (or the first season, depending on your poison). It's a looming question and threat we're yet to fully grasp. The answers don't begin to appear until much later in the series.

First half

In the first half of Star Wars, how proactive is Luke in going after what he wants (to join the Rebellion and make a difference)?

He's not proactive at all. Every decision he makes in the first half is forced upon him or made for him because it's the only realistic option, or because he has other concerns holding him back from going after what he wants.

Why?

Because he doesn't believe in himself and what he wants strongly enough. He still wants it, but he's reluctant and reactive rather than determined and proactive.

He's forced to make a life-changing decision only when his Aunt and Uncle are murdered, but even then he's not proactive. Events have pushed him onto the path that will take him to what he wants, but he's still reluctant to walk it.

What about the movie Pretty Woman (AKA Cinderella). What does Julia Roberts' character Vivian want in the first half of that movie?

She wants the dream. The perfect life.

Does she know she wants it? Not really, but she does know she wants more than what she has - a better life than being a prostitute.

Is she actively doing anything to get it? No. It's a wish. A distant dream she can't even articulate.

Going to work for Edward puts her on the path to getting what she wants. It opens opportunities. It's not until she's shown Edward's amazing life that she begins to understand what she wants, and realises it could be possible to get.

From your character's perspective, they would rather there wasn't a problem - and so they start off reluctant and reactive.

Whether they wish something was different or not doesn't make a difference. There may be good reasons for your protagonist not to take action in the first half (people they care about may be hurt if they rebel, for example, so they do nothing no matter how badly they want to change their situation). This makes them reluctant to act.

In Pretty Woman, the main question is common to all romances: Will they get together? Or more to the point: How will they get together?

Such questions don't have an easy answer, but the story would be boring if it did.

Second half

In Star Wars, after the Millennium Falcon arrives at the Death Star, Luke begins to become proactive. The discovery that Princess Leah is a prisoner spurs him into action, and Luke convinces the rest of the group to help rescue her.

In Pretty Woman, Vivian is living the high life, and to her surprise discovers she likes it.

She also begins to believe that with a little effort she can fit in. Her physical appearance has changed, and on an emotional level she's changing drastically. She's found a life she wants to be a part of, and even though she recognises it as a fairy tale she's no longer a pawn of circumstance.

She wants the dream, and one way or another she's going to change her future. That means answering the questions raised in the first half and standing up for what she wants.

Overall, the two halves reflect your protagonist's changing attitude and help form their character arc.

They've realised the situation isn't going to get better unless they actively change it. No one's going to give them what they want, so they have to do it themselves. It's what resonates with audiences.

Your protagonist must accept their situation and become proactive about it, largely by seeking answers to the questions raised in the first half. If done well, those questions should align with what they want.

All things considered, your protagonist would avoid the tough events and choices if there was a simpler, easier way to get what they want.

But there isn't. You must take them on a *difficult journey* where they're *forced to deal* with the problem.

If you haven't seen Pretty Woman and Star Wars, grab copies and check them out. They're worth studying.

You should also check out successful books like Dune, the Harry Potter series, Twilight, the Hunger Games, The Girl with the Dragon Tattoo, and anything else that's sold in the millions and hundreds of millions. Try the movies instead of the books if you prefer.

Additionally, watch other popular movies and plays, and read graphic novels.

Popular stories resonate on many levels and across mediums.

Structurally, they all work in the same way. Emotionally, they engage their audiences.

Character wants

Start with figuring out what your protagonist wants. If you know what they want you can figure out ways to ensure they're held back from trying to get it early on, and ways to ensure they become more proactive about it later on.

Some examples from stories you probably know:

- Marlin wants his son back (Finding Nemo)
- Neo wants to break the machine's hold on humanity (The Matrix)
- Ferris Bueller wants another day off school (Ferris Bueller's Day Off)
- Harry Potter wants to stop Voldemort from getting the philosopher's stone (Harry Potter and the Philosopher's Stone)
- Paul Atreides wants to break the Padishah Empire's grip on the galaxy (Dune)
- Bella wants to be with Edward (Twilight)

If those examples are too specific, consider them in terms of genre. The protagonist wants:

- to solve the crime
- win the heart of their lover and live happily ever after
- save the world.

As a quick mental exercise, try to come up with a few more broad examples similar to these. You're probably thinking 'what about...' already.

Once you've got a broad understanding of what your protagonist wants, apply it more specifically. For example, a:

- surgeon may want the support of their hospital to try an experimental procedure in order to save a patient's life
- politician may want to get specific legislation through parliament that will benefit millions of people
- kid may want to win a competition
- dog may want a home
- a pirate might want to find the greatest treasure that ever existed.

These are end game wants. How you, as the writer, deal with these wants at the beginning depends on your story.

The essential thing is that your protagonist must want it - desperately - by the second half of the story at the latest. The more they want it, the stronger the conflict and drama, and the greater the emotional response you can get from your audience.

Let's apply this to a simple fantasy scenario where a farm boy has to stop an evil empire from taking control of the world. That's the basic plot for a large number of fantasy novels, but also for one of the most successful movies ever: Star Wars.

What does Luke want?

He wants to destroy the Empire and make the galaxy a better place. Breaking it down, he wants to join the Rebellion and make a difference, but can't because of his farm duties.

Character needs

Didn't we just do this?

Um... no.

Wants and needs are very different. Consider them akin to star-crossed lovers. You can't have one without the other, yet they're from different worlds.

The difference is that wants are external and needs are internal. Additionally, a character can't get what they *need* until they get what they *want*, and they usually get what they want around the three quarter mark. Getting what they want never fulfils them, however, because what they want is external.

What they need is internal, like confidence or some sort of resolution enabling them to move on, for example.

In the case of Star Wars, Luke *wants* to join the Rebellion and make a difference. He gets to join the Rebellion around the three quarter mark.

What he *needs* is to believe in himself, and it's only during the assault on the Death Star that he comes to believe in himself and he's able to destroy the super-weapon.

In Pretty Woman Vivian wants to fit into Edward's world, and she achieves that around the three quarter mark, blending in to the point where only people 'in the know' would pick it.

It's not what she *needs*. She *needs* to actually belong for the fantasy to become real, and she can only get that if Edward's willing to take the final step and marry her.

Early on, Vivian's friend Kit tells Vivian she doesn't belong on the streets as a prostitute, that she doesn't fit in, and never did. Its fantastic foreshadowing.

When Vivian finally comes to understand this truth, that on an emotional level she's not going to be happy living on the fringes of Edward's world, she holds out for the real deal, determined to walk away and create a new life if she can't have it. She *needs* to find inner strength so she can determine her own fate.

Putting it into practice

Think in terms of conflict - there's usually some form of internal, external or interpersonal conflict holding your protagonist back in the beginning - doubt, fear, the enormity of the problem, circumstances, naysayers, etc.

Initially it's easy for your protagonist to avoid these problems and not to put themselves out there. For the story to happen, a push or some form of incentive is usually needed.

This is their journey, and it's both physical *and* emotional. You can't ignore one and get away with it.

Your audience also expects a logical story (so they can understand it) and an emotional story (so they can feel it). Wants and needs.

It's the emotional story that's the most important part, but for the emotion to work they've got to understand it. A house isn't a home until you make it one.

Consider your story in relation to your protagonist:

- What questions will your story raise in the first half?
- How will your story answer them in the second half?
- What holds your protagonist back in the first half?
- Why do they become proactive in the second half?
- What do they want early in the story?
- What do they need to be fulfilled by the end of the story?

7

QUARTERS

Hopefully you've got your two halves sorted from the protagonist's perspective.

You should also have a solid understanding of the story's main conflicts and how they influence your protagonist.

Now it's time to break the story down.

Write four headings:

- Setup
- Adventure Begins
- Things Get Serious
- Resolution

Every romance, for example, has the same structure:

- they meet (Setup)
- they romance (Adventure Begins)
- they lose each other (Things Get Serious)
- they get back together (Resolution).

You could take the same approach with any genre. For example, a murder mystery:

- Murder/mystery (Setup – a murder/mystery causes an investigation)
- Investigation (Adventure Begins – investigation begins in earnest)
- Failure (Things Get Serious – they close in, but don't catch the bad guy)
- Justice (Resolution – justice prevails)

How all that happens is the important part, and different genres have different rules and tropes.

For example, a fantasy story often follows some sort of a quest scenario, but it doesn't have to. It can just as easily be about a romance or a murder mystery or a war, incorporating any number of other genres. It will still work as a fantasy as long as it includes fantasy tropes such as magic and/or magical creatures.

Despite that, it will still have the same basic structure:

- a setup
- the consequences of the setup begin the adventure
- once the protagonist has learned enough the adventure will get more serious
- a final resolution.

First quarter - Setup

The purpose of the first quarter is to:

- show your protagonist as they are in their normal world
- demonstrate why going for what they want is a difficult path
- throw some kind of change at them, forcing or encouraging them to take their first steps out of their comfort zone.

Even a protagonist who is desperate for change can be confounded by barriers which make change difficult - internal or external.

A protagonist might want to take their kids on a holiday, but real-world issues such as a money issues, a busy job or marital problems could cause difficulties.

Because of those barriers, a family holiday may mean risking everything, with the consequences of failure outweighing any potential benefits.

In Star Wars, Luke's sense of responsibility to his Aunt and Uncle outweigh his desire to do what he believes is right - join the Rebellion and fight the Empire. This holds him back. He could leave at any time and sign up for the Rebellion despite his Aunt and Uncle's wishes, but he chooses to stay and help on the farm instead. If he believed in himself a little more he might have joined the Rebellion despite his obligations.

Instead, it takes circumstances beyond Luke's control to push him out of his farm life.

In Pretty Woman, Vivian wants a better life, but she doesn't know what that life is in the beginning of the story. Because of that, she finds herself unhappy and with no way forward, and so she's forced to continue living the same life in order to make ends meet.

It's not until she meets Edward that she's given a glimpse of a world she both disdains and wants to be a part of, and finds the courage to escape where she was.

When Edward offers her a temporary solution to her problems (money for a week with him), she's quick to accept.

Breaking it down

There are three plot points you need to hit in the first quarter of the story. The:

- Inciting Incident
- Call to Adventure
- Fateful Decision

We'll get to these soon, though I've already touched on them in the above examples.

At this point, you only need to consider one question:

- What is going to change and make your protagonist choose a new path?

As the writer, it helps if you can make that choice a difficult one. The more difficult it is, the more your audience will empathise.

Take some time to think about it and possible alternatives, even if you're sure you know what it is. Brainstorm at least ten possible scenes/ideas/concepts that could bring change to your protagonist's normal world. Twenty would be better.

Write them down in bullet points and pick the one you think will best serve your story. Add that to your development outline.

Second quarter – the Adventure Begins

As the title says, the second quarter is where the adventure actually begins.

By this point your protagonist has chosen to have an adventure of some kind (investigate a murder, get involved in a relationship, or destroy an evil overlord), perhaps due to forces beyond their control. Whatever the reason, *they've decided*.

That means they could have chosen another path such as to go back and rebuild the destroyed farm (Luke in Star Wars), or turn down a business proposition (Vivian in Pretty Woman).

Instead, they choose to go to Adventureland.

What this means is that your protagonist now finds themselves in a situation they're not familiar with and you've got to make it interesting for your audience. This is also where you, as the writer, get to have fun.

Your protagonist's now out of their depth. Make the most of it.

If it helps, think of it as a fish out of water situation where your audience is learning along with your protagonist.

For example:

- Luke explores Mos Eisley and the space cantina. (Star Wars)
- Vivian discovers how the other side live. (Pretty Woman)
- Ferris Bueller ropes his friends into the next phase of his planned day off. (Ferris Bueller's Day Off)

Your protagonist's new outlook might include anything, such as; politics, a new business venture, entrance into another culture or level of society, or even a whole new world or universe (or all of the above).

They must explore and learn. This is their training ground. The threat's not too serious yet, but it's going to escalate and you need to prepare them for it.

It's also a place for audience entertainment. Make it fun (for your audience, if not your protagonist).

Show your audience your protagonist's potential as well.

They may be out of their depth, but they're adapting. Put them in situations they need to master. If your protagonist already knows everything about their new world they're not going to be interesting. At best they'll be the mentor, not the protagonist.

Instead, they're the student, and so is your audience. They need to learn and grow.

In Star Wars, Obi-Wan demonstrates the Force when he uses his mind control skills on a couple of Storm Troopers, as well as his lightsabre skills (foreshadowing Luke's potential).

In Pretty Woman, Vivian learns to appreciate the life of the filthy rich.

In a movie like The Matrix, Neo learns martial arts and what's possible within the virtual world.

In any murder mystery, the audience and the protagonist develop an understanding of the killer's world and why they're doing what they're doing.

In any romance, the couple get to know each other while the groundwork is laid for them to fall in love.

In a fantasy, the protagonist learns something fantastical – the potential of magic, for instance.

No matter your genre, this is where the fun happens. The threat's not overwhelming yet, and the antagonist's not close enough to do any real damage.

Entertain your audience.

Putting it into practice

At this point, ask yourself these three questions:

- What cool events or situations occur?
- What does my protagonist learn from that will help them in the end?
- How can these situations be most effectively used to entertain an audience?

Third quarter - Things Get Serious

The third quarter of your novel is when the story takes a major turn for the dramatic. Your protagonist has learned a few things and become more proactive, but the threat is now closer to being realised.

In terms of structure, this is where they go up against their 'enemy' more directly. It's often a warm-up to the final battle, where:

- their mettle is tested
- they fail to resolve the problem

In more specific story terms:

- the lovers break up
- the antagonist gets away
- victories don't stick and may even make the situation worse.

While these situations are all very real for the protagonist, what matters to the audience is how it affects the protagonist emotionally.

There's a reason the mentor/teacher character gets killed or sidelined here – it's a signal to the audience the protagonist is about to take full responsibility for their situation. Having someone forever hold their hand isn't good for storytelling.

Emotionally, this quarter represents a low point for the protagonist and sets them back. It hurts them, but it's supposed to.

The same thing is represented in different ways with different types of stories. The murderer gets away. The army loses a battle. The lovers quarrel and break up.

Everything they'd hoped to achieve is in doubt at this point, and emotionally, your protagonist needs to know this, and care about it a lot.

Additionally, there's not likely to be an obvious way forward (or at least not an easy one). The more real that appears to your audience, the better.

Fourth quarter – Into Battle

The final quarter is all about fighting for what they believe in, beginning by reassessing the situation and coming up with a new strategy before shooting for the win. Your protagonist should be very active now – leading the action or at least in the forefront of it. Before this point, they may have had a win and seen it come to nothing, or they might have taken a good hiding and have been forced to rally.

Whatever the reason they're here, this is their last chance. If they fail, they'll never get another chance. Your audience needs to know that.

In almost any action movie, it means suiting up and trying again. In a crime story, a new lead may result in fresh evidence and a win in court. A romance means taking another shot at getting back together.

In the case of Star Wars, it means analysing plans and attacking the Death Star. In Pretty Woman, it means taking control of your own future and holding out for the fairy tale.

In short, your protagonist makes a whole new plan, implements it, and fights for victory in a last ditch effort.

Putting it into practice

- How does your protagonist use what they've learned?
- How will they win?

8

THIRDS

Thirds... thirds is a bit of misdirection, really.

Still, we are talking about the three main parts of your story, the: *beginning*, *middle* and *end*, so it's not unreasonable to assume they'd be equal in length.

They're not.

While each part has its own distinct role to play over the progress of your story, they come in two different sizes.

We're really talking about two quarters and one half - but not in that order.

Three parts, disproportionate sizes.

In case you're a numbers person, a balanced story's structure is roughly based on its word count or screen time, and when expressed as percentages should be close to:

- Beginning: 25 per cent
- Middle: 50 per cent
- End: 25 per cent

Read on, it'll all make sense in a moment.

9

THE BEGINNING

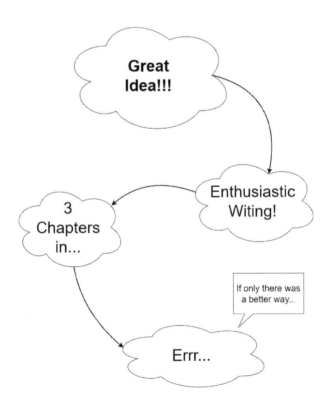

The beginning is equal to the first quarter, the middle is half the story overall, and the end is the final quarter.

The question is: why are they disproportionate?

Think of it like a season of sports.

- Your protagonist goes to tryouts and signs up: Beginning.
- Weekly training and regular season games: Middle.
- They get to the playoffs: End.

Like a season of sport, the bulk of the story's in the training and season games.

It's easy to assume they'd be a third each, but they're not. The middle is half the total story.

If you like, pretend the middle turned into a thug and beat up the beginning and end in order steal some of their more entertaining bits - yet got the boring bits instead (or so it would seem to many writers).

Let's turn that thinking around 180 degrees.

In the beginning, the adventure hasn't started yet - the middle and the end are where the actual adventure takes place.

So if the beginning's not part of the adventure, what's the point?

Your audience isn't born familiar with your characters or your story world. You need to introduce them, the situation, and the problems your characters are going to face.

The beginning is the first quarter of the story, but 'story' and 'adventure' aren't the same thing.

You're prepping your audience, which means you must:

- educate your audience on what's considered normal for your protagonist
- highlight what the problem is
- get them to root for a protagonist who's about to have an adventure.

In the case of a sequel, you may be able to tweak this somewhat, but it will still have its own problem, and that means taking the time to set it up.

A really great example of this is the movie Serenity - the story that followed the short lived cult-classic TV series, Firefly. Joss Whedon, the writer and director, had to assume the history of the story wasn't known to the entire audience despite the earlier television series, which came with two challenges:

- to entertain the people who *were* familiar with the show
- to educate the people who *weren't*.

The challenge of entertaining and educating is the problem you face every time you begin a story, whether it's the first in a series or a sequel somewhere down the track.

You can't assume people know anything; backstory, story world or real-world history, or even the genre's tropes and creatures (not everyone knows everything about vampires for example), and definitely not your characters.

Every time you begin a story, even a follow-on sequel, you need to:

- introduce your characters so your audience knows who they are
- showcase your story's world and its rules
- introduce the story's main problem
- entertain your audience while doing all of the above.

Putting it into practice

- Who are your main characters and how will you introduce them?
- What's unique or special about your story world, and how will you let your audience know about it?
- How will you introduce your story's problem?
- Are the answers to the above questions going to entertain an audience?

10

THE MIDDLE

The middle is the part of the story that sags for many writers, largely because so many writers don't know what it's supposed to do. The question often is: 'How do I fill the gap between the start and the finish?'

It's a tough question. How do you take your reader from the creative, interesting, squeaky-newness of the introduction all the way to the epic and glorious finale?

What does the middle actually need to accomplish?

Essentially, the middle is your protagonist's preparation for bigger problems, covering the second and third quarters of your story. These two quarters forge your protagonist into a hero, teaching them what they need to know in order to win whatever battle they're up against (whether that's a love rival, a psychotic killer, an evil overlord etc.).

The middle transitions your hero from bamboozled neophyte to qualified journeyman ready for their trials of mastery.

The middle is their schooling, their training ground, and a place for less-serious skirmishes and battles. It's not the war.

They start with support and grow to stand on their own.

It's about attitude, transformation and skillset creation. This may include:

- changing your protagonist's outlook
- beefing up their physical skills
- developing their knowledge.

By the end of the middle, your protagonist must come to the realisation that, "if it is to be, it's up to me". This change is reflected in the action of the story and forms a major part of your protagonist's character arc.

Putting it into practice

Ask yourself:

- What must my protagonist learn that will help them resolve the story's main problem?
- How will they practice/employ what they've learned
- How can I demonstrate this to my audience?

11

THE END

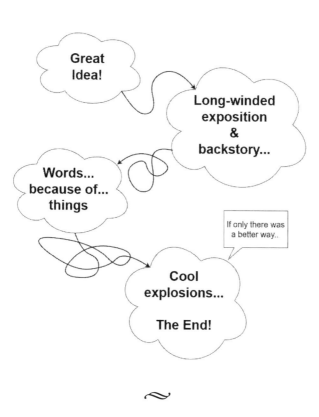

If you've set the story up correctly, in the beginning you'll introduced your characters, their story world, and the main story problem.

Throughout the middle, you'll have trained your protagonist and given them some practical experience.

Now it's time to give your audience the ending they've been lead to expect.

The end is where your protagonist puts it all together and fights for what they believe in, no matter whether that's true love, a world free of tyranny, or happy puppies with wagging tails.

To do this, they'll have to figure out how. They've most likely taken a few hits already, or had the air deflated from their heads after realising they'd had a victory or setback that wasn't final. This means figuring out a new strategy and giving it everything they've got – this is their last chance and their final hope. Everything's on the line now, and there's no second chances.

In Star Wars, Luke jumps into an x-wing along with a bunch of other Rebel fighters to take on the Empire's heavily-armed and armoured Death Star, a moon sized military base a squadron of x-wings would normally have no chance against. He's armed with a couple of photon torpedoes, his x-wing's lasers, and a little bit of knowledge about a potential weakness in the Death Star. He's seriously outgunned and up against an opponent (Darth Vader) who has far greater skills and experience than he has.

In The Matrix, Neo goes on a rescue mission to save Morpheus, his mentor, from the artificial intelligences who guard The Matrix. Armed with newly-developed martial arts skills and the knowledge The Matrix's rules can be bent, he loads up with as many weapons as he can carry and goes on a suicide mission to save Morpheus.

In Pretty Woman, Vivian, having learned the etiquette and rules of life in Edward's world, now realises she was never really a part of it. Yet Vivian still wants 'the fairy tale'. With no wealth of her own and having realised she can no longer accept half-measures and live only on the edge of Edward's world, she decides to forge her own future. For her, either Edward forks out for a wedding cake and marries her, or she'll leave him. This is her stand, her fight, and it's the only real power she has. She wants the fairy tale, and if she can't have it she'll take her sexy lingerie and go home.

In Twilight, Bella understands what vampires are capable of and the special abilities of those she's involved with, but she's drawn the attention of James, a vampire who wants to kill her. While Edward and his family rally to protect Bella, she knows she doesn't have a chance alone against her pursuer, and running from James is only drawing the people she cares about into the conflict. Using her knowledge about the vampires protecting her, she escapes their protection to confront her pursuer alone, hoping to save the people she cares about most.

Putting it into practice

- How is your protagonist going to apply what they've learned in order to resolve the story problem?

12

THEME EXPRESSED

Story themes are tricky beasts to corner, but integral to character choices and how the story unfolds and resolves.

Without a strong theme your story is just a series of escalating events which will soon be forgotten.

The true power of theme, however, has more to do with *who you are* than the story you write. We'll get to that in a moment.

While you don't have to pin a theme down right away, it helps to be open to any hidden gems you might discover during the planning or writing phases. Those gems will unify your story and give it meaning, at least to you.

Conversely, you could write half a dozen drafts before discovering what you're trying to say with your theme.

So what exactly is a story's theme?

Let's try a quick exercise

Think about what you believe your story's theme is (pick the most important one in your story if you think you have several).

- Write it down.

Seriously, write it down. This is important. We'll revisit your answer soon enough.

It's all about theme

Have you ever:

- read a book or seen a movie you've instantly forgotten?
- finished a story and thought it was entertaining, but it wasn't good enough that you wanted to tell anyone about it?
- had someone ask you about a story you recently read or experienced, but you couldn't remember what it was about off the top of your head?

The story probably lacked a strong theme. Such stories tend to drop out of conscious thought as soon as they're finished.

Why?

Because they're not saying anything worthwhile.

In your case, assuming we're talking about your story, *you're* not saying anything worthwhile.

Your theme is your message, your opus, the entire point of your story. Without a theme, your story is as meaningful as an action movie that relies on special effects and body-counts for impact - quickly forgotten.

Your theme makes a statement about the topic your story is exploring. For example, in a story about a flawed genius who finds love, the statement may be: "The brain is the sexiest part of the body." Your story would then argue for or against that statement. It's that simple.

If the theme doesn't fit, keep working on it - or change your story to fit. Either way, your theme is in there, you just have to find it. It'll be something that matters to *you*.

Most writers struggle with the concept of theme, usually referring to concepts like 'love', 'hope,' 'loneliness,' 'loss,' or 'regret.'

They're aspects of your theme, but not themes alone.

Theme isn't a metaphor. Metaphors may be strong expressions of your theme, but they don't encompass all of it.

Your theme is a topic for debate or questioning - it's your argument about a given subject.

The problem is, while single words are often thematic, they're not actually themes. They're motifs.

So how would you define a theme? Simple:

- **Your theme** is a *statement* or a *question*.
- **Your story** is the playground where you *demonstrate* it.

Two sides of a coin

Theme:

- *influences* story events
- *is the message* you're imparting through the story.

Story:

- *illustrates* the theme
- *serves* the theme.

For example, your theme might be: "You can never truly be yourself around your family." Your story would debate that statement (representing both sides), with everything in the story eventually demonstrating that the statement is either true of false.

56

Another way to look at is is to ask it as a question: "Can you ever truly be yourself around your family?" Your story asks the question and demonstrates it conclusively.

"Who am I?" might be a good theme for a biography or autobiography. The story would ask and answer the question... by showing who you are over the course of the story.

And that's where the power of a theme emerges; it's what gives your story real-life meaning and keeps readers thinking about it long after they've experienced the story, even if they don't have a clue what the theme actually is.

Theme forces people to think about your story, and consequently it's probably the most understated, least understood, yet most powerful part of any story.

Where do you begin when considering theme?

Theme is a powerful tool, so begin with what you want to say about a topic.

Theme:

- adds (hidden) depth to a story
- defines your story's deeper meaning
- is your story's message.

Take the song Cats in the Cradle by Harry Chapin. Look it up on YouTube, search the internet for the lyrics, buy it or stream it, whatever, but check out the lyrics and the question of theme should become clearer.

Cats in the Cradle is a story of *regret* - but regret is only an expression of the theme. A motif.

Family features strongly throughout the song, particularly the father's relationship with his son, but family and relationships aren't themes either. They're motifs as well.

The *story* is about both, but the *theme* is so much more.

Cats in the Cradle is a cautionary tale of missed opportunities and poor choices, and the theme *illustrates* the consequences.

So what exactly is the theme? Read on.

In your story, your theme should influence everything your characters say and do, but don't force a theme if you don't have one straight away.

Once the story's planned or drafted you still have time to figure out the theme and, where necessary, go back and align your story to it. Don't forget – story serves the theme, not the other way around.

At the planning stage, defining a theme can be about pointing the story in a direction; writing down a question or statement you think you may want to explore. If the story's not going where you expect, keep an eye out for a more compelling theme. It'll probably appear naturally, so don't try to force it. Merely try to see what's already there, inside you and on the page.

Possible themes could be anything, including:

- Eternal youth is a curse, not a blessing.
- Broken trust can never be completely healed.
- What's truly important can never be stolen.
- What does it mean to be human?
- You must be true to who you are.

As far as the story goes, the theme you need to find is the one that reflects your protagonist's story arc. For an ensemble cast, the character most closely aligned with the theme represents your protagonist.

The way to test your theme and whether it's going to work is to turn it into a question.

- Is eternal youth a curse or a blessing?
- Can broken trust ever be completely healed?
- Can what's truly important ever be stolen?
- Should you always be true to who you are?

Turning the statement into a question lets you see both sides of the debate. If you give your audience both sides of the debate and bring your story to a logical conclusion based on how it plays out, it's harder to be preachy (assuming you're fair to both sides and treat it like a true debate).

Back to Cats in the Cradle. If you were to write a theme for Cats in the Cradle, what would it be?

- Write it down (yes, now).

Theme's place in a story

Plot is:

- what happens in a story
- a logical progression of events based on *audience expectations.*

Story is:

- about your characters - the reason your audience cares.

Theme is:

- why plot and story matter - *the deeper meaning.*

What *insight* are you trying to provide through your story? What are you trying to say about:

- a person in particular?
- people in general?

- the world at large?

This should give you a clue about what your story is actually about as opposed to what happens.

Understanding theme is easy once you know what you're looking for.

Understanding theme and how it's applied gives you a huge advantage, putting your story on a better footing than most.

And that's all theme is - whatever you want to say about a topic. It's your insight into something important to you.

Preachers be warned!

Don't preach. Nobody wants to be preached to.

You can get away with preaching to your choir (if you have one), but beyond those already sold on your theme you need to *demonstrate* its truth, not preach about it.

If we were to take preaching literally, 'God is great!' is a strong thematic statement. Use it if it fits your story and you want to prove it true or false, but if you do then your story must *demonstrate* exactly why the statement is true or false. Illustrate your point with such finesse that your readers don't even realise you're telling them something important.

'All men are bastards.' Sure, that's a strong theme too, and totally appropriate if that topic is important to you, but your story needs to demonstrate that it's true - or prove the statement's wrong.

'Life is cheap.' Again, a perfectly fine theme, but how will you show your audience just how cheap life is - or if arguing the opposite side, demonstrate the true cost of treating life cheaply?

Make your theme touching. Make it angry. Make it a part of a story people will remember for all the right reasons. Make it emotional. Make it a question you want to explore. Make it something you care about.

Cats in the Cradle

So what's the theme for Cats in the Cradle?

- 'You reap what you sew.'

Revisiting the quick exercise from the beginning of this chapter

In the first exercise, what did you write down as your theme?

- How would you change it now?

Putting it into practice

- Write down at least one topic you care about.

Turn it into a statement or question. It must be:

- a topic you can argue, or
- a question you can answer, and
- demonstrable by your story.

13

THE STRUCTURAL ELEMENTS

When I first started writing fiction, I called my epic fantasy kingdom Fandelion. I wanted something distinctive yet pronounceable.

I was surprised when I realised people were pronouncing my special word entirely wrong: Fan-de-lion instead of Fan-del-yon. The word in my head hadn't translated very well to text.

Telling people how it was actually pronounced got a range of responses, mostly of the rib-poking variety, yet for me it was a significant problem. I was attached to the word and I wanted it pronounced correctly, so I changed the spelling from Fandelion to Fandelyon, assuming that would sort it out.

It didn't work, and I didn't have a clue how to fix the problem. My one and only solution was a failure.

That's the problem with words, ideas and stories. Words are designed to transfer thoughts from person to person, but they're far from perfect at doing it. When writing, every word has to be translated at least twice - from an author's thought into writing, and then back into the reader's mind. Add additional collaborators such as directors, producers and actors, and there's a lot of room for interpretation just in a single word. Considering the difficulties in finding the right word let alone the right way to tell a story, the chances are you'll never get any idea or concept across exactly as you want people to experience it.

That's where structure helps. Without some sort of structure your story will be a complete mess. Words have structure. Sentences have structure. Paragraphs and scenes and chapters have structure. Stories need structure - it's a necessary evil.

Fortunately, people are familiar with how stories work, so if you work to those expectations you'll reduce misinterpretation and more accurately represent your story the way you'd like it to be understood.

Structure and creativity

Story structure has a reputation for restricting creativity by imposing artificial limitations on art. There's some very good arguments for this, but most are about avoiding responsibility for meeting an audience's expectations, and for blaming the audience if the story fails.

The simple fact is, audiences need at least a basic level of structure. Without structure they won't understand your story – it'll be a mess to them.

As a writer, it's your responsibility to apply creativity to your story's structure. If your audience doesn't understand your story it's because you don't understand your audience, not the other way around.

Only fools lay blame, so figure out how your audience thinks and feels and reacts, and write your stories in a way they'll be more likely to appreciate.

You'll do better by giving them what they want – a story they can understand.

And that's where structure is applied to creativity.

Structure is simply a series of story points that have been known to work in the past. Use them, or at least understand them so you can justify why you're breaking convention. While most experiments fail, some succeed with incredible results.

That might be you.

The difference between professional and amateur writers is simple:

- A professional writer understands their audience and accepts responsibility for their own successes and failures.
- An amateur expects audiences to understand their work and assigns blame if they fail.

Usage

The structural elements in the following chapters are known to work for audiences, but don't interpret that as a list of lazy checkpoints to be ticked off as you write, or as a simple crutch for hacks. Structural points are about audiences, not writers.

Understanding why they're important and how to use them creatively will help you meet expectations, and these days audiences have pretty high expectations. You may be able to get away without using only some of them or by making very little of specific points, but these points resonate with audiences.

Ignore your audience at your own risk.

Story elements

I've mostly chosen movies as examples of the following story structure elements, partly because movies are easy to get a hold of and experience for yourself, but also because they're often good examples of story structure being applied. Once you have your own copy of a movie you can re-watch and analyse it repeatedly. It's a great way to learn.

I strongly recommend getting copies of the examples I've used and watching them as a companion to this book.

It helps to be able to see the examples yourself rather than trying to visualise the explanations, or remember the examples after watching a while ago.

I've used a range of stories and genres, as well as a few that appear to break the mould at first glance.

14

THE INCITING INCIDENT

The Inciting Incident is the part of your story where something stands out from the day-to-day, but alone doesn't alter the status quo. It's a normal part of the protagonist's world. It could be as simple as a friend dropping by or hearing news about the outbreak of war. Their lives haven't changed but it heralds change (even if they don't realise it at the time).

The inciting incident doesn't need to stand out in any significant way, but with hindsight its significance becomes clear.

The inciting incident is one of those structural elements that's easily overlooked, particularly in plot-driven stories such as a zombie apocalypse. The apocalypse will happen regardless, and so the inciting incident can seem superfluous to requirements.

It's not about meeting a plot point, it's about foreshadowing. In the case of a zombie apocalypse, it might be as simple as a news broadcast hinting at a new flu outbreak that's spreading rapidly.

The inciting incident is about letting your audience know the situation's about to change, and dropping a hint to the protagonist. The protagonist may or may not see it as anything but routine, but that's your choice. If they're a scientist trying to convince authorities there's a global disaster coming, they'll champion the inciting incident (and usually not be believed). If they're not interested in or aware of the coming change, they'll probably ignore it.

Either way, it's a portent, your first hint at an adventure.

In order to make the inciting incident work, you'll need to give your audience some sort insight into what's normal for your protagonist – their day-to-day lives. That can often be challenging because normal is often boring.

It doesn't have to be, but there's plenty of ways to ensure it is, and this is usually due to a lack of conflict. You're setting up an adventure, after all, not delivering one.

Try to find conflict based on the world building/situation rather than contrive it through unrelated issues, like interpersonal conflicts that have nothing to do with the main story problem.

Your ability to demonstrate an interesting 'normal' provides a reason for your character to want to resolve the story problem, as well as a baseline to give contrast later on. This contrast becomes very important for making your audience care when events and situations begin to go wrong for your protagonist.

You can certainly skip the inciting incident and other structural elements if you like, but skipping story elements that audiences have come to expect reduces empathy and understanding. If you throw your protagonist into the adventure straight away you're giving up insight into what your protagonist is fighting for. Without a baseline to establish what's normal outside of the adventure, the adventure becomes the norm and your audience won't appreciate their reasons for fixing the problem.

What then is your protagonist fighting for? Another adventure? If you can't show they care about anything outside of the adventure, then what's the point of giving them an adventure in the first place?

Skipping these structural steps is often justified by writers creating plot-driven stories. For instance, an apocalyptic event such as a meteor striking the Earth or a zombie apocalypse. What's normal at the beginning can never be normal again, right. So what's the point in setting up 'normal'?

Normal is about establishing your protagonist's care factor. What do they care about prior to the apocalypse? Friends? Family? Knowledge? Whatever it is, that's what you've got to setup so your audience knows it's worth fighting for.

Ignoring these early 'setup' structural elements is more likely to occur in action-oriented stories, but few, if any, leave a lasting impression. That's because the threat isn't significant enough.

It's a problem that needs to be solved. So what? Your audience can't care about the broader consequences if you haven't established any.

If you want to engage your audience, don't skip this step. Even in a dystopian story like the Hunger Games where the characters have little or no say in what happens to them, these elements are the main reason the story worked so well.

With the Hunger Games, the approach of the Reaping served as the inciting incident. For an audience it was essential as it foreshadowed the events to come for Katniss Everdeen, the story's protagonist.

The yearly Reaping was normal for Katniss, but with hindsight it was clear that change was coming and something was going to be different afterward. The same can be said for almost any story that resonates with an audience. It could be anything:

- A couple meet for the first time. *Normal, but different.*
- A stranger arrives in town. *Normal, but different.*
- New equipment is installed at the office. *Normal, but different.*
- Your protagonist gets an unexpected invitation. *Normal, but different.*

The announcement that a country has declared war may act as an inciting incident, but alone the announcement doesn't change the character's situation, even if it changes how they feel about it. The war may get called off, leaving your protagonist without an adventure.

The inciting incident is the herald of change, not actual change.

You're not necessarily going to tell your audience what that change will be, but it's a clue.

Examples

Although most of these examples have been around for a while, they do contain spoilers, so you might like to stop here and check the stories out before continuing.

Cast Away

Cast Away is the story of a man named Chuck (played by Tom Hanks) who runs his life and his business affairs by the clock. He's about to find himself with nothing but time and next to nothing to fill it with.

The Inciting Incident arrives while Chuck's celebrating Thanksgiving with his fiancé Kelly (played by Helen Hunt) and family. Chuck's pager goes off, an unwanted interruption. It's a normal part of Chuck's life, but the timing is inconvenient.

This incident is made significant by the look Chuck receives from Kelly. It's a disruption, heralding the start of Chuck's adventure.

Ferris Bueller's Day Off

Ferris Bueller's Day Off is a very interesting story. It *appears* to break from what's considered a normal story structure, but on closer inspection it still follows story structure very closely, making it a good example of how to play with the appearance of structure and get away with it.

It also misdirects beautifully. It's not a story about Ferris at all. He's not the protagonist. He's more of a mentor or trickster rolled into one, like the love child of Obi-Wan and Bugs Bunny. It's a clever way of appearing to break the mould while heavily relying on it.

While Ferris Bueller drives the story and action, it's the characters around him who carry the emotional arcs and define the theme.

You have to look to the other characters to figure out whose story it really is.

The Inciting Incident happens *before* the opening credits. Ferris has already decided to take the day off, and so the story opens with him in bed, faking illness to put his plan into action. It's enough to fool his parents and get him the day off, but his sister, Jeanie, doesn't buy it, and his best mate, Cameron, is about to find out how much Ferris's choice is going to affect him.

Happy Death Day

Happy Death Day is one of the many iterations of the classic movie Groundhog Day. The concept has become something of a genre in itself.

Groundhog Day and its homages are usually mysteries at heart, and the fact that it's the same day over and over appears to 'break the formula'. Yet, as with Ferris Bueller's Day Off, this appearance is cosmetic. Groundhog Day-type stories still comply with standard story structure and audience expectations, something you'll need to do if you want to break the formula yourself.

Happy Death Day is a fun take on the genre, yet still carries the emotional punch and structural beats necessary for any successful story.

The Inciting Incident in Happy Death Day is subtle, largely because it's a representation of a situation already in play before the story starts, and the beginning sets up this groundwork and hides it well.

The Inciting Incident occurs in a brief scene at the hospital when

Theresa 'Tree' meets her roommate Lori, who works at the hospital. Lori clearly states that what Tree is doing at the hospital will have some serious consequences (we find out what Tree's at the hospital for in the next scene), but the earlier groundwork cleverly disguises the importance of this scene, so it's easily overlooked.

Miss Congeniality

Miss Congeniality is one of those movies that, when casually glanced at, should probably have never worked, or at least come across as 'just another one' in the comedy genre. However, it carries a strong emotional punch and delivers on the promise of a light-hearted comedy while going well beyond it.

The Inciting Incident in Miss Congeniality comes when the FBI is sent a letter from a domestic terrorist threatening the upcoming 75th annual Miss United States beauty pageant in San Antonio, Texas. For the FBI it's 'business as usual', but for the audience and the story's characters, it heralds the point of the movie.

Monsters Vs Aliens

Monsters Vs Aliens is an animated kid's movie and, on the whole, kid's stories are usually pretty well structured. You could pick almost any animated movie to break down and find most 'stick to the formula' pretty tightly.

There's no real reason to pick Monsters Vs Aliens over any other animated story, but the humour makes it fun to watch and review, so it's in.

The Inciting Incident happens well away from Earth and the protagonist, Susan (Gigantica). The antagonist Gallaxhar blows up his home planet in an effort to steal and control its quantonium. As far as Susan's concerned, nothing's changed, but for the audience its clear changes are about to take effect.

This inciting incident is a good example of breaking the mould, as it appears to have nothing to do with the protagonist. The important thing is, it happens, and it's going to be significant.

Pretty Woman

The Inciting Incident in Pretty Woman arrives via a sports car. Edward is lost and Vivian offers to give him directions... for a fee.

This is a star-crossed lover's romance – two people from very different worlds coming together despite the odds (and in this case, social norms).

At this point in the story they haven't entered into any kind of a relationship. It's the 'cute meet' part of the story, and an indication their relationship is about to commence.

While neither Edward nor Vivian have done anything they would consider outside the realm of their normal behaviour, the fact that Edward, a wealthy businessman, picks up Vivian, a penniless prostitute, and takes her to his hotel is a pretty strong signal to the audience.

Star Wars

Star wars plays with The Inciting Incident a little, in that the first hint of it is when R2D2 and C3PO arrive at Luke's farm – a long way into the beginning of the story.

The droids' arrival isn't The Inciting Incident. The Inciting Incident comes when R2D2 runs away because the droid has been tasked with getting the plans of the Death Star to Obi-Wan Kenobi.

Luke's world hasn't changed, but the incident threatens to get him into trouble with his Uncle, and he needs to find R2D2 before that happens.

Matrix

In The Matrix, The Inciting Incident occurs when Trinity contacts

Neo via his computer, telling Neo to 'follow the white rabbit'. It's an iconic part of the movie.

On its own, it appears as if Neo's computer has been hacked. Unusual, but still within the realm of 'normal'. It's just a message, after all. Neo can act on it or ignore it.

His world hasn't changed, but something's certainly different. Having the message arrive via computer is a hint to the audience that the story will be about computers, or artificial intelligence, as it may be.

Twilight

Twilight plays with the inciting incident too.

Initially, Bella and Edward are forced to sit next to each other in class. There's nothing unusual about two students sitting next to each other, but Edward's behaviour is a little odd as far as Bella's concerned.

He's not friendly toward her, and bolts the moment the bell rings. This is also the 'cute meet' part of the romance where the two lovers come together for the first time.

In this case, the meeting leaves Bella both curious and a little offended by Edward's behaviour. Something isn't right, but she's not sure what it is. Nothing's changed about her world, at least not that she's aware of, but it's a mystery.

The real inciting incident comes when Bella nearly dies in a car accident. Fortunately for Bella, Edward is there to stop the car crushing her to death. The problem for Bella is that stopping the car should have been impossible, yet Edward did it anyway. Her curiosity is fully piqued now.

Putting it into practice

There's no need to limit yourself to what you can do with the inciting incident.

All you're really doing is setting up a coming change. You're not altering the rules of that world or upsetting its natural order. You're merely foreshadowing the adventure to come.

- What are you going to introduce to, remove from, or otherwise foreshadow in your story world during the inciting incident?
- How does this affect the story (without changing what's 'normal')?
- How does your protagonist act or react?

15

CALL TO ADVENTURE

Your protagonist will get a chance to have an adventure (usually) late in the beginning part of your story. Your job as the writer is to make that decision as difficult as possible for them in order to derive empathy from your audience. If it's a tough decision, people will care. If it's not a tough decision, that's okay too, but the care factor you have an opportunity to generate will be reduced.

The call to adventure could come in almost any form. Your protagonist could:

- get pushed/forced into action (the need to rescue someone, for instance).
- get a request for help.
- face a difficult choice based on their own needs or desires.
- confront an obstacle that was holding them back.

Or you could apply a bit of reverse psychology - have a bit of fun.

- They could receive an ultimatum to *stay out of* something.

No matter how the call to adventure arrives, it must arrive with inherent conflict.

- What will it cost your protagonist to accept the call?
- What will it cost if its ignored?

Put another way, a choice without options presents no conflict for your protagonist. The call to adventure works best if you present a difficult problem with inherent consequences or benefits.

In The Hobbit, going on an adventure with a sorcerer may have been what Bilbo Baggins secretly wanted, but to do so would cost him a considerable amount of standing in the community - something he valued a lot. That made the decision difficult.

To give your protagonist a compelling call to adventure, put a huge cost on it if you can.

Examples

Cast Away

In Cast Away, the call to adventure arrives at the same time as the inciting incident. It's disguised as a call to work which Chuck feels obligated to answer. If Chuck knew the significance of it, I doubt he'd have accepted.

Regardless, the call gives him a choice: go to work and miss dinner and disappoint his fiancé, or ignore the call and keep his fiancé happy. It's a difficult choice, but duty wins out.

Ferris Bueller's Day Off

As already stated, Ferris Bueller's Day Off is not about Ferris, but in a nice twist it's told from his perspective. So whose story is it?

It's primarily his sister's story (Jeannie's), though the bulk of the movie focuses on Cameron and his role as a second protagonist.

What Ferris Bueller's Day Off does is give us the illusion of a protagonist (Ferris Bueller), while delivering two storylines with two protagonists. Their journeys are told simultaneously and interwoven with Ferris's adventure, cleverly disguising what's really going on. All the right beats are in all the right places, despite the fact there's two story events running simultaneously.

Ferris doesn't receive the call to adventure – he provides it. He's the instigator, not the protagonist.

So who gets the call? Initially his sister Jeannie while Ferris is faking illness to get the day off. Right then and there she sees him 'getting away with it again', and when he gives her a conspiratorial wink you can see from her expression she desperately wants to do something about it. It's as much a challenge as a call. In another nice twist, it also appears to set her up as the antagonist.

The next call to adventure is far more traditional – Ferris literally picks up the phone and calls his best friend Cameron, demanding Cameron have an adventure with him.

Happy Death Day

Like Cast Away, the call to adventure in Happy Death Day comes in the same scene as the inciting incident and the following fateful decision.

The call to adventure is a twist on the concept in Happy Death Day, in that reverse psychology is used. Rather than being offered an adventure, Tree is warned off having an adventure by her roommate Lori.

Of course, being the selfish, self-centred person Tree is, she isn't in any way influenced by the warning.

Miss Congeniality

Gracie Hart, the clumsy FBI Agent who's determined to help out on 'The Citizen' case, gets her chance in a fun scene where, courtesy of a little software and FBI stock photos, she finds herself cast as the only person with the right appearance to enter the Miss United States pageant - young, good looking, and with a body to match.

The competition is everything she detests - the exploitation of beauty over brains. It's her worst nightmare, and a very difficult choice.

Monsters Vs Aliens

After having captured Suzan, General Warren R. Monger enters the monsters' common room with an announcement; they're all getting out of there. There is a catch, however. They have to defend San Francisco from an alien robot. The adventure is waiting and Suzan has a dilemma – she wants her freedom, but doesn't want to do what it's going to take to get it.

Pretty Woman

Pretty Woman plays with the call to adventure. The first call is when Edward makes Vivian an offer of paid sex to come up to his room. It's a simple business transaction that works for Vivian, so she accepts. An easy decision. It keeps her on the path to her fateful decision.

It's not the real fateful decision.

The second and more profound call comes when Edward offers her a full week's work. This is the real call to adventure, and has the potential to solve all of Vivian's short-term money problems. The trade-off is a week of her time.

Star Wars

Luke balks in Star Wars when Obi-Wan Kenobi calls him to adventure. For Luke, answering the call would force him to neglect his duties, and as a hero that's not a good look. He doesn't want to let his Aunt and Uncle down as they need him on the farm.

The Matrix

The Wichowskis played with the call to adventure in The Matrix; they gave Neo three chances to turn it down.

The first time he's called, he surrenders to The Matrix's agents rather than accept the call to adventure.

The second call gives him the option to remain with Trinity and meet Morpheus, or leave. He chooses to continue the adventure, but it isn't the real decision - it merely keeps him on the path.

The third time he receives the call to adventure, his options are represented by a red pill or a blue pill: the chance to find out what The Matrix was all about or walk away forever. This is it, and it's clear there'll be no turning back once the decision's made.

Twilight

In Twilight, the call to adventure is akin to the one used in Happy Death Day – a push away from adventure rather than a call to it, but it has the same effect.

It arrives when Edward refuses to tell Bella what had happened during the car accident. This isn't what Bella wants to hear. She wants answers.

Putting it into practice

However you play it, there must be a choice offered during call to adventure, a decision they have to make. The more difficult, the better for your story.

Ask yourself:

- What is your call to adventure?
- What are the consequences of saying no?
- What are the consequences for saying yes?

16

THE FATEFUL DECISION

The name makes this part of the story obvious: the protagonist chooses their fate following the call to adventure. The fateful decision gives them this choice and generates the consequences of that choice.

Play the game or go home. Do something about the zombie apocalypse, or hide and hope it blows over. Whatever it is, the option to have an adventure is on the table and protagonist must choose what they're going to do.

In reality, the choice is a foregone conclusion. Your job as the writer is to make it appear as if it's a real choice, and the protagonist can still avoid getting off their butt and taking the harder road. And it is a harder road.

The easy option is avoid it, but no matter what they may want, they know what they have to do.

The fateful decision essentially puts the protagonist on the path to dealing with the story's main problem. Until the fateful decision is made, the option to ignore the story problem remains available. They haven't committed to anything yet. But they're going to – they just don't know it yet.

Consider yourself the evil overlord in this scenario, and you've a pen full of ink and you're willing to use it.

Of course, the fateful decision doesn't have to be life-threatening or even all that unappealing, though it does need consequences. It's the fork in the path your protagonist needs to choose from.

Robbing your protagonist of choice means you'll be seen as nothing but a chess master moving pieces around a board, and that's no fun for an audience. Your audience needs to be invested in your characters, not your cleverness. That may mean your protagonist's circumstances would be dire if they say no, but the option still has to be there for them.

Choices and consequences are the difference between getting your audience on side with the characters and their plight, or giving yourself away as a puppet master dragging your protagonist around the story world on a predetermined path.

Even if your protagonist has no little choice about an event that's out of their control (such as the asteroid about to strike Earth, or a war), how they deal with it is what matters, and that means giving hem choices. The choice may be as simple as run or fight, but unless you give them agency, your audience is going to struggle to care.

Examples

Cast Away

Again in Cast Away, the fateful decision is also part of Chuck's Thanksgiving dinner. He's been called to work. Chuck, being the company man, chooses responsibility despite the fact his fiancé wants him to stay, and puts himself on the path to an unexpected adventure. He didn't choose an adventure, but he was given the choice to stay home. If he had, there wouldn't have been no adventure. Story over.

Ferris Bueller's Day Off

As this story has two separate storylines tied to Ferris Bueller, it has two Fateful Decisions.

Jeanie's fateful decision comes while she's at school, long after Cameron makes his own Fateful decision. Prompted by the antics of the other students who are fundraising to 'save Ferris', she decides she's not going to let him get away with his day off. She's going to catch Ferris out and expose him as a fraud.

Cameron, after receiving the call to adventure from Ferris via a good old fashioned phone call, is now at war with himself. He doesn't want to answer the call, but he knows Ferris will keep pestering him until he does. He eventually gives in to the call to adventure and drives to Ferris's house where the next stage of Ferris's scheme begins.

Happy Death Day

Like Cast Away, in Happy Death Day the inciting incident, call to adventure and fateful decision all arrive in the same scene.

What's soon to be revealed is that Tree is on her way to have sex with one of her professors, and in the call to adventure her friend Lori warns her off the affair. Tree ignores the warning and makes her fateful decision to continue her affair.

Had Tree changed her mind right then and there, things might have turned out very differently, but she chose the affair and as a consequence, the adventure.

Miss Congeniality

Gracie Hart initially refuses the call to adventure. She doesn't want to be in a beauty contest. She detests them (as the story demonstrates). She values her career more.

Entering the pageant is her only opportunity to restore her damaged career however.

Although still at war with herself, she makes her fateful decision and accepts the call to adventure, entering the pageant as a fake contestant.

Monsters Vs Aliens

Susan and the other monsters are dropped off on the outskirts of San Francisco to fight the robot probe, yet Susan hasn't committed yet. She's along for the ride, but hoping things will work out so she can claim her freedom without doing anything.

At an offer from Dr Cockroach she runs and hides, but that's when things go south for her.

The robot probe is actually after the quantonium she's imbued with, and it's only when regular people are threatened that she makes her fateful decision and takes on the robot probe. Although she doesn't really have much of a choice about the events she's caught up in, she has a choice in how she handles them. In this case, she takes the fight to the robot probe instead of hiding.

Pretty Woman

After Vivian stays the night, Edward makes her a new offer – stay for the week and he'll pay her more than she's likely to make in months.

For Vivian, the fateful decision is easy - she needs money. Although she could easily walk away, she negotiates on price and accepts his offer. There's only one proviso – no romance. The deal calls for a business transaction only, and that's a strong hint to the audience about what the story problem is going to be.

Star Wars

Luke's been offered a call to adventure: to go with Obi-Wan to Alderran.

Due to his responsibilities and emotional connections to his Aunt and Uncle, he initially turns the offer down. In this case he needs a push, and with the offer still on the table, Storm Troopers kill his Aunt and Uncle.

At that point he could have stayed and rebuilt the farm if he'd wanted to, but he chooses to have an adventure with Obi-Wan instead.

The Matrix

The Matrix has one of the clearest Fateful Decisions you'll ever come across.

Neo is offered a red pill (adventure) or a blue pill (no adventure). It's the difference between answering the question about what the matrix is, and losing the answer forever. He doesn't know the full consequences the offer will bring if accepted (what protagonist does?), but he does know what he wants at that point in the story. He takes the red pill and has an adventure.

Twilight

The fateful decision is a demand from Edward *not to have an adventure*, but Bella's curiosity and interest in Edward have already been awakened.

Despite the push-back from Edward, Bella wants to know how Edward saved her. Deciding to pursue that question represents the first step on the path to adventure.

Putting it into practice

Books tend to have a different pace to movies. The budget for special effects and settings in books is unlimited and it's easier to get into a character's head. Movies, conversely, have tight deadlines and limited budgets.

Additionally, the author of a book only has two people to please - themselves and their ideal reader. That gives authors more freedom about when and how events play out. It also means that on the whole, books are not as tightly structured as movies and many other forms of entertainment.

However, the most successful books tend to be closely aligned with a standard story structure. That includes a fateful decision.

Ask yourself:

- What decision does your protagonist make in order to define their adventure?
- What are the costs of their decision?
- What are the potential rewards?

17

THRUST INTO NEW WORLD

Your protagonist has made a decision to have an adventure and to take on whatever challenge they're presented with. The main story problem may not be apparent yet, and your protagonist may not be happy about their decision, but they've made it anyway.

The more difficult you can make it to turn back, emotionally or physically, the better. There's even a good chance your protagonist resents the necessity.

Story structure is a bit like NASCAR racing – almost everything about each car is defined before it's even built, but despite that some NASCAR teams build them better than others, while others never get it right. The difference is the crew and the driver, not the parts.

You're the driver and your crew are your characters, beta readers and any other people who have a hand in your story's creation.

This part of the story is an awakening for your protagonist. Things are now different, and turning back may no longer be an option.

It's about perspectives. By this point your audience knows what's normal for your protagonist and what matters to them. This section pushes your protagonist into unfamiliar territory, and like anything new, it comes with emotions like fear, joy, and hope.

How your protagonist reacts at this point is far more important than the unfolding events and scenery.

That means they're facing change, and change means conflict. Whether they want an adventure or not, they're going to do things they've never attempted before, and they're going to react emotionally. If you do it well, your audience will empathise.

It's complicated because you're dealing with human emotions, both real and imagined. How are your characters going to feel and react? The answers are going to depend on them and their situation.

- Have they just entered into divorce proceedings after spending twenty years with their partner?
- Have they graduated from school and now entering the workforce?
- Have they made a new enemy they need to deal with?
- Are they physically different – become a superhero for instance, or perhaps been in a car accident and now have to deal with limitations they never had before?

Whatever the change to their circumstances, this is their new reality and they need to take responsibility for it - perhaps now, perhaps later.

There may still be an option to return to how things were. If they're a kid and have run away from home for instance, they may be able to return home. The problem is, the circumstances that drove them to run away haven't changed, and going back may be the worst possible choice for them.

Going back might be possible, but you need to make sure it's not viable.

Examples

Cast Away

Chuck is quite literally thrust into a new world - marooned on an isolated island with absolutely no help or people to rely on. He has no mentor and few survival skills. All he has when he washes ashore are the clothes he's wearing, his wrecked blow-up raft, and some boxes.

He needs to learn how to survive.

Ferris Bueller's Day Off

It's time to make the day meaningful. For Cameron, this means taking his father's Ferrari without permission. It's a showpiece, not transport, and taking it thrusts Cameron into a whole new world he's not prepared to deal with.

Jeanie, meanwhile, has faced the reality that her brother is pulling the wool over everyone's eyes, and she's the only one who can see it. She goes to the office to see the Principal about it, gets rebuffed, but it only spurs her on. She leaves school, determined to catch Ferris out.

Happy Death Day

The Groundhog Day 'genre' of stories is very clear on this part of the story. A mystery is presented to the protagonist when they wake up from death (usually) and they experience intense déjà vu. It's the same day or moment they'd experienced earlier, which is impossible under normal circumstances. Regardless, they have to deal with it.

In Tree's case, she's just been murdered, yet she wakes up in Carter's dorm room again, making her think she had a really bad nightmare. It's like she's losing her mind... and so the day repeats. Tree's entered new territory, and she's about to discover what that means for her.

Miss Congeniality

Gracie Hart meets Victor in preparation for the Miss United States pageant. It's clear in the meeting that she's completely out of her element and has a lot to learn very quickly if she hopes to fit in.

For Gracie, that means a complete makeover.

Pretty Woman

Vivian has embarked on a week living the life of the rich. She's in Edward's penthouse, not her run-down apartment she shares with Kit. Life is looking up, particularly when given money to go shopping. It turns out that life is life, and despite access to money she still faces the same prejudices she faced as a prostitute. It's time to learn how to fit in.

Star Wars

Luke goes to Mos Eisley, a world that's only a little familiar to him. Farming's been his whole life and largely all he knows – big cities and their challenges are new to him. Circumstances have forced his hand however, and now he's about to experience a lot more than farm life, beginning with an encounter with Storm Troopers. To survive the coming adventure he needs to learn, and that begins in Mos Eisley.

The Matrix

After taking the red pill, Neo wakes up aboard the Nebuchadnezzar - and it's too much for him. The real world isn't the reality he expected. He loses it and the contents of his stomach at the same time.

There's no option of going back for Neo no matter what he wants - it's simply not possible. He's no longer hardwired into The Matrix, and he doesn't know what that means yet. He has a lot of adjusting ahead, but that's what he's there for.

Twilight

Bella, now curious, seeks answers to the mystery surrounding Edward. She has no idea what she's getting into, but she's determined to figure out how he saved her life. That means research.

Putting it into practice

When your protagonist goes from their normal, comfortable world into the new, unfamiliar world, they learn things. This knowledge creates emotions - joy, devastation, enthusiasm, fear.

Everything gets far more complicated at this point - how your protagonist reacts is entirely different to how any other person would react. You need an understanding of people to ensure your protagonist doesn't act out of character.

Ask yourself:

- What specifically changes for my protagonist?
- How do they deal with it?

18

EXPLORES NEW WORLD

Your protagonist has made the decision to have an adventure and now they've landed in a world they're unfamiliar with. That means they're a long way from being equipped to deal with the main story problem.

If they're already equipped to deal with the problem, then you'd better rethink your story. If it's not a struggle, it's not interesting. The greater the struggle and the more your protagonist has to fight to attain it, the better the audience engagement.

By this stage of the story your protagonist may have allies or friends they can rely on, and perhaps even someone holding their hand during these first few baby steps, but how much support you give them is entirely up to you.

Make them figure everything out on their own if circumstances dictate, but without a support cast you'll need to become inventive - Wilson the volleyball from Cast Away comes to mind.

Whatever your protagonist's new situation, for you as the writer this means fun (and if it doesn't, reassess). This is where you get to show off your story world at its best and worst.

Demonstrations (as opposed to explanations) are in order.

It's a perfect place to give your support cast free rein so your audience can see what they're made of, and perhaps an inkling of what your protagonist could become.

The story's main threat isn't serious at this point. The problem is still a long way from being your protagonist's main concern. Surviving and learning are their main priorities at this point. This is true even for stories that don't rely on action, such as a romance. For example:

- A kid at a new school needs to learn the ropes.
- A medical practitioner may need to sort out a new bureaucracy or research an illness they've never seen before.
- A castaway needs to learn how to survive.

Whatever your scenario, this is where your protagonist develops the skills enabling them to succeed in the end.

It's their education. It may be a brutal education where they'll learn resilience, or a friendly education by people they care for and trust. It could be the best time of their life or the worst, but they will learn, and it will equip them to deal with the story problem.

As well as showing your audience what's possible, here you get to teach your protagonist personal traits or physical skills they're going to need.

From a writer's perspective, it's also where you educate your audience about the new story world and what's possible, using your protagonist who learns along with them.

Cast Away

Survival is at the top of Chuck's 'to do' list, and although he's poorly equipped for it he's obviously seen a documentary or two and has the brains to know where to start.

This part of the story is exclusively about Chuck learning to survive on the island; find food, make shelter and create fire to cook fish and crabs. There's triumphs and failures, but on the whole he gets there.

Ferris Bueller's Day Off

Ferris and Cameron get Ferris's girlfriend (Sloan) out of school, ready to hit the big city for a day of adventure. On their way they drop the Ferrari into a parking garage before going for lunch at an upmarket restaurant, and the adventure begins in earnest.

Jeanie leaves school and discovers Ferris isn't home. She's in for a surprise because there's an intruder in her home, and it's up to her to deal with the problem.

Both protagonists are out of their depth and in an adventure they're not prepared for. For Cameron it's fun. For Jeanie, it's terrifying. Both are learning things about themselves they didn't want to know.

Happy Death Day

Tree, after waking up and very much alive, is in disbelief. She's reliving the same day, but tries to pass it off as déjà vu. Although she does things a little differently and avoids a mistake or two she made the previous day, she gets killed once again, only in a different place and way.

And then it happens again... and again... and again. With every death she learns a bit more about what's happening and why.

Miss Congeniality

Gracie finds herself well out of her depth as a crew of beauty specialists prepare her for the Miss United States pageant.

Despite her name, she has no grace and no talent (for the talent part of the event), and has to learn quickly. Its makeover time and she needs a lot of making over.

Monsters Vs Aliens

Susan defeats the gigantic robot probe with a little luck and a lot of heart. It's enough to secure her freedom and so she and her fellow monsters return to her parents' home to celebrate. It's party time and everything looks good, but then the party goes south thanks to the social inadequacies of her new monster friends, and her fiancé Derek dumps her because he doesn't want to be overshadowed, showing her his true colours.

It's a harsh education, but she finally begins to understand she can never be normal now - she's changed too much, and she no longer fits into the world she was once familiar with. She hasn't yet embraced her differences but accepts she's no longer the same.

Pretty Woman

Vivian discovers the world of money and just what can be accomplished with it. Following a disappointing solo shopping expedition where she's humiliated by shop owners, Edward teaches her just how much respect money can buy when he takes her shopping.

It teaches her to respect the power of money and what it can do for her, and she discovers she likes it.

Star Wars

Luke learns about the Force thanks to an unexpected demonstration by Obi-Wan upon entering Mos Eisley, where Obi-Wan uses mind control to convince Storm Troopers they're not looking for the two droids with Luke and himself. It's a glimpse into Luke's future and what he'll be capable of.

It's also the place where the other characters show their skills and characteristics – Han's ruthlessness and the droids cunning, both of which Luke will need to use later in the story.

The Matrix

Neo learns about The Matrix, what it is, why it's there, and how to bend its rules.

He also learns martial arts which he'll need later in the story. His training is visually spectacular, and it's something he embraces despite the fact he doesn't always come out on top.

Twilight

Bella pursues her interest in Edward, growing closer to him in the process through a series of awkward interactions. Eventually, she discovers his vampire secret, and rather than running from it, she embraces it.

Putting it into practice

- What are you going to reveal to your protagonist about their story world?
- How will you reveal it?
- How will it benefit the protagonist?
- What is your protagonist going to learn about themselves or the world?
- How are they going to feel about it?
- Why are these things important to your story?

19

MIDPOINT

The midpoint is both a turning point in the story and a change in tone for the events that follow. Similarly, it signals a change in the protagonist's attitude. They're about to go from reactive to proactive.

Your protagonist's apprenticeship has taught them the basic skills they'll need for this exciting new world. At the midpoint they should have learned enough to start to get by. They're not yet a master, but they're no longer a complete novice either. It's enough for now, as they're up for some challenges they wouldn't have been able to take on in the beginning of the story.

In short, they've grown as characters.

The midpoint is the perfect place to throw in a major plot twist and turn the story completely sideways. Throw an unexpected challenge at them, destroy a tightly-held belief, or betray them, just so long as its not something they're prepared for.

From the midpoint, the story's main threat must get more real and personal - demonstrate it if you can.

In something like a romance, the story's midpoint often points toward someone who doesn't want the couple getting together, whether that's the mother-in-law who disapproves of the relationship, a rival, or even a well-meaning best friend.

If it's an action story, your protagonist's probably in for a surprise. The bigger the surprise, the better.

The protagonist of a crime story might get their first real lead here.

Whatever your genre and the story's scenario, we're about to catch a glimpse of the hero in transition from 'wannabee' to 'gunnabee'. They're not there yet, but the midpoint shows their transition from defence to offence.

This turning point might be forced upon them through circumstance or it may be a choice based on their own morals and attitude, but whatever it is, they're becoming more motivated to stand up for what they believe in.

Discovery, learning, and the fun that goes with it may still be contributing factors to the story after the midpoint, but they no longer drive the story forward.

The midpoint and the next quarter of the story must remind your audience that the story problem hasn't gone away and the threat is growing.

If your protagonist doesn't start doing something about it, they'll fail.

Examples

Castaway

In Castaway, Chuck has learned to survive on the island, but surviving is no longer enough. He could, quite literally, survive on the island indefinitely now that he's mastered survival skills, hoping to be picked up by some random ship or spotted by a low flying plane. It's been years though, and he realises rescue is highly unlikely. He's done with waiting.

The midpoint signals Chuck's changing attitude. It's time to find a way off the island. He just needs the right opportunity.

Ferris Bueller's Day Off

Ferris has successfully fooled his parents into letting him take the day off. He's conspired to involve Cameron and Sloan in his deception, and appropriated Cameron's father's Ferrari.

It's time for the personal problems to come out amid the escalating adventure. They're heralded when Cameron and Sloan discuss their futures after high school.

Jeanie, on the other hand, needs help dealing with the intruder in her home, and calls her mother and the police to no avail.

Happy Death Day

The midpoint arrives when Tree wakes up from yet another death and immediately collapses. A couple of hours later she wakes up in hospital where she's shown some X-rays and told she shouldn't be alive.

There's evidence of physical trauma inflicted from her previous deaths, which has left scar tissue and other damage. Every time she returns from death, she bears the consequences, meaning she has limited lives before the bodily trauma becomes too great.

The midpoint here signals that time is running out. She may not have unlimited lives like she thought she did, and for the first time she's made aware that the clock's ticking.

Miss Congeniality

Gracie has gone through a transition to make her presentable for the pageant. It's now time to do what she's here to do: enter the pageant. She looks hot but she's still clumsy. It's enough to fool the other contestants and allow her to infiltrate their ranks. Now it's time to put what she knows into practice. The only problem is, what she knows isn't suited to her new situation, so she'll need to adapt.

Monsters Vs Aliens

Susan is depressed. Although she's won her freedom, she can no longer return to her normal life. It's a crisis point and she has no direction. Right at that moment she gets beamed up into Gallaxhar's ship while her monster friends are left behind.

The event turns the story in a newer, far more dangerous direction, and she'll need everything she's learned up to this point to survive and save Earth.

Pretty Woman

The midpoint transition comes when Edward is alone and playing a piano in a closed dining room. Vivan goes to him even though she's not obligated to. The relationship has developed to the point where she now genuinely cares for him, but she doesn't admit to it. It signals a change in their relationship.

Star Wars

The midpoint in Star Wars comes when the Millennium Falcon blasts out of Mos Eisley space port, dramatically changing the story landscape from desert world to space. It represents a new phase in the story, as does nearly being caught by the Empire. Things have gotten a lot more dangerous.

The Matrix

Neo's training is done and Morpheus has made a decision: they're going to go and see the Oracle.

This increases the risk and means danger for the group as they're entering the real Matrix and the threats it brings.

Twilight

The midpoint of Twilight comes when Edward reveals himself in sunlight to Bella - the sparkly vampire scene everyone loves to deride. What it does however, is signal a change in their relationship - a certain level of trust and a genuine desire to be with each other. From this point on they're together, showcasing Bella's transition from outsider to being part of the family.

Putting it into practice

- What changes demonstrate that things are getting more serious?
- What is the first thing your protagonist does to demonstrate they're now more proactive?

20

ALL IS LOST

All is lost and the darkest hour are often two halves of the same event, although they're very different in practice.

The *all is lost* moment is a physical event or situation, while *the darkest hour* is emotional. That's a very important distinction as it's also the difference between a plot point and a character moment.

All is lost comes first, and it often (but not necessarily) drives how the darkest hour plays out. They're usually very tightly linked in this regard.

In a romance, this moment usually arrives when their relationship falls apart and one or both of them get hurt. How that happens is irrelevant from a logical perspective, but very relevant from an emotional point of view when the darkest hour comes into play.

In an action story or thriller, the all is lost point arrives when their main plan gets shredded and there seems to be no way to get back on track and achieve the win.

In something like a murder mystery, the murderer will probably get away with their crime despite everything looking good for the protagonist up to that point.

It's also the place where a key character is likely to get killed (if it's that kind of story). This event drives the ensuing emotional impact (darkest hour) arising from their loss. The loss of such a significant character is what allows your protagonist to step into the vacuum and take on the responsibility of coming up with a new plan and seeing it through.

However you look at it, whether through the eyes of a heroic adventurer, the tension of a thriller or the hopes and dreams of a romance, the all is lost moment is where everything falls apart for your protagonist. There's no clear path forward.

No matter what your protagonist expects to happen, it goes sideways instead. The future they hoped for is lost. The bleaker the situation appears, the better (at least as far as keeping your audience guessing and engaged).

Additionally, the greater the build up to a hoped-for future, the more impact you'll deliver when you upend everything.

Examples

Cast Away

Chuck has decided to risk everything to escape the island. He builds a raft and literally casts his chances to the wind. He knows the likelihood of survival is slim, but the alternative is worse; remaining on the island until he dies of illness or injury, never seeing another human again. He wants a life, not an existence, and the island can't give him a life.

Eventually Chuck launches his raft and leaves the island, but all his preparations come to nothing as he drifts on the ocean. He runs out of supplies, his raft slowly begins to break apart, and he sees no land nor any sign of rescue. He realises he's not going to be rescued and will die on the ocean. All is lost.

Ferris Bueller's Day Off

After a great day out without getting caught, Ferris realises the Ferrari's odometer is showing well over a hundred more miles than it should. Cameron, up to this point happier than he has been in years, freaks out at the news. Even if they get away with everything school-wise, he's going to have to face his father over the Ferrari issue.

Jeanie has landed in the police station for making a false call for help. It's the worst imaginable result for her. Instead of catching Ferris and getting justice, she's now the one in trouble. There's nothing left to do but wait for her mother to come and pick her up.

Happy Death Day

The all is lost moment comes when Tree finally believes she's figured out who her murderer is. It's the psycho killer being treated at the hospital. Everything has fallen into place except for one small glitch. In the ensuing chase/slasher scene, her wannabe boyfriend Carter saves her life, but in doing so gets killed himself.

Despite figuring out the mystery, she's out of options. If she kills her murderer and resets the day, Carter will be dead for good.

Miss Congeniality

The investigation is being shut down. The Citizen has been apprehended (apparently), and so the threat to the pageant is over - or so Gracie's bosses believe.

Gracie is certain the threat comes from a copycat, and argues for the investigation to remain open. Nobody believes her, and the investigation is shut down anyway.

Monsters Vs Aliens

Susan, trapped aboard Gallaxhar's ship, gets caught in an extraction device and the quantonium is removed from her body. She returns to her normal size and strength, everything she'd wanted earlier in the story, but it means she's now powerless to stop Gallaxhar. She's lost her only chance to prevent the invasion.

Pretty Woman

The all is lost moment in Pretty Woman is handled a little differently to many other romances. While there's no rival fighting for either Edward or Vivian's emotions, the threat to their relationship and Vivian's fairy tale coming true is that their business deal is coming to an end and isn't going to be renewed.

After spending a wonderful day with Edward, Vivian finally admits to herself that she loves him as she lays awake in his arms, but remains powerless to prolong their relationship. With only one more day together, she accepts the fact that their relationship is over.

Star Wars

The plans to get off the Death Star go well initially. Obi-Wan turns off the traction beam and Luke, Han and Chewie get Princess Leah out of her prison cell, but then everything goes wrong. Imperial troops corner Luke and his companions in the prison corridor and the only way out is the garbage chute. The all is lost moment arrives when the garbage compactor is turned on while they're trapped inside, threatening to crush Luke and his companions to death.

The Matrix

Neo and his companions have seen the Oracle and everything us going okay, but on their return Neo notices a glitch. They've been betrayed and find themselves trapped and surrounded, with no way out of the building. They're going to be captured or killed.

Twilight

In Twilight, the all is lost moment arrives when the vampire James threatens Bella's life. There's a good chance Bella's father, Edward or another member of Edward's family could also be killed.

Putting it into Practice

- What plans, hopes or dreams did your protagonist expect to realise?
- How are those plans, hopes or dreams destroyed at the all is lost moment?

21

THE DARKEST HOUR

The darkest hour follows the all is lost moment, but unlike the all is lost moment, it's not necessarily a plot point. It's emotional.

It often relies on the fallout your protagonist experiences following the all is lost moment. While they don't necessarily need to be tied together, they often are.

As an emotional point, the darkest hour can signify the loss of the protagonist's hopes, such as when their plans for success get dashed.

It's an emotional kick to the head delivered with the protagonist's inability to see a future where anything could work out.

If your protagonist is going to hoist a white flag and surrender, this is the moment. The more devastated and emotionally shocked they are, the better. Your protagonist may even be contemplating tearing up their flag into strips and using it for something darker.

However you do it, it's got to be emotionally painful for the protagonist. Often this involves the loss of someone or something they desperately care about. It could be:

- the realisation a relationship or friendship is over
- a betrayal by someone they thought had their back
- a close friend's death.

The possibilities are endless, so get creative.

Whatever the trigger, your protagonist must care about it because if they don't care they can't be hurt. If they can't be hurt there's no emotional impact and no darkest hour. It's your protagonist's care factor that makes this such a powerful point in the story.

Examples

Cast Away

In Cast Away, the darkest hour comes when Chuck realises he's not going to make it. He's adrift on a raft which is slowly falling apart, there's no hint of land, and his outlook is bleak. He's dying. His darkest hour is represented on-screen when he loses Wilson (a volleyball he talks to as if a real person). After this point he gives up. His dreams of getting home are gone and he's not far from death.

Ferris Bueller's Day Off

After Cameron loses it at the news his father's Ferrari has been driven without his knowledge (all is lost), he's devastated, and goes into a funk. His father loves the Ferrari more than he loves Cameron, and Cameron fears the consequences. It's like his life is over and he wants to die. The devastation he feels is his darkest hour.

Jeanie has been picked up by the police for making a false call when she reported an intruder in her home. She's now at the police station, waiting for her mother to come and pick her up. It's the worst thing that could have happened - she wanted to catch Ferris out, but she's the one paying the consequences. To rub salt into the emotional wound, a kid brought into the station for drugs has the gall to tell her the whole situation's her own fault.

Happy Death Day

Tree's devastated at the loss of Carter. He's her only real link to a normal life if she ever gets out of the murder loop. In essence, he represents the life she wants to resume. If she kills her murderer, it means Carter' gone for good and she'll never get her happy ending, even if she escapes the loop.

Miss Congeniality

Although Gracie stands up for her beliefs as she's sure the pageant's contestants are still in danger, no one backs her, least of all her partner. It's devastating, because above everything else, she values her job and the respect of her colleagues.

Her boss, exasperated, gives her permission to stay, but she'll have to do so as a private citizen, not an agent. Staying could cost her career. She chooses to stay regardless, knowing she's alone from this point on.

Monsters Vs Aliens

Susan's in deep trouble. She's Gallaxhar's prisoner and has lost the quantonium which gave her giant size and strength. Without it, she's just a regular human and no match for Gallaxhar. Her darkest hour comes as Gallaxhar tells her his plans; his clone army is about to conquer the Earth, and everyone she cares about will soon be dead. Her own fate looks just as bad. She's about to be incinerated.

Pretty Woman

Vivian now realises she's fallen in love with Edward and is about to lose him forever. This leads to her darkest hour - the fairy tale is over and she's facing life as a prostitute again, something she'd hoped to put behind her.

Star Wars

In Star Wars, the darkest hour the death of Luke's mentor, Obi-Wan, heralds Luke's darkest hour. Obi-Wan's death leaves Luke in the company of a smuggler and a woman he doesn't know, and the likelihood the Rebellion is about to be crushed by the Death Star. Even worse, Obi-Wan was the Rebellion's only hope, and Luke's not able to fill his mentor's shoes.

The Matrix

In The Matrix, the loss of Morpheus due to Cypher's betrayal triggers Neo's darkest hour. They've lost most of their crew and everything looks hopeless. This is demonstrated when the machines begin breaking into Morpheus's consciousness. When that happens the machines will have everything they need to destroy humanity. For Neo, it's the realisation the Oracle was right, and he can only save Morpheus if he sacrifices his own life.

Twilight

Forced to leave Edward and her father thanks to the threat James poses, Bella realises there's a good chance she'll never see Edward again. This is her darkest hour, her greatest fear, and there's absolutely nothing she can do about it. She's helpless to influence events or do anything to protect the people she loves.

Putting it into practice

- What event or realisation triggers the darkest hour for your protagonist?
- What are the emotional consequences for your protagonist?

22

FALSE VICTORY/DEFEAT

Your audience loves a good twist or turn, and this is a perfect place.

The term false victory/defeat may seem fairly self-explanatory, but isn't quite that simple. There's a victory, or a defeat, but they're not the final victory or defeat.

The trick is to sell it to your audience and convince them the situation's real.

Additionally, following on from the all is lost and darkest hour moments, how could you possibly have a victory? Alternatively, why would you want to dump yet another defeat on your characters? Haven't they been beaten down enough?

The false victory/defeat is more about toying with expectations than any win or loss.

It keeps things interesting. It ensure's the conclusion's not foregone and there's still room for surprises. It's a great place to twist the situation around completely.

Your protagonist might win a battle but quickly realise the war is still raging, or they may lose their lover only to discover there's still hope.

More to the point, this is the battle they think *is* the war, and so any win or loss means they need to rally and fight again. The battle's lost or won, but the war isn't over.

Whether they win or lose the current fight isn't relevant from a plot perspective, but it matters to the audience because your characters need to care. Winning the battle may mean simply surviving to fight another day, while losing it could give you a chance to demonstrate their resolve and show them picking themselves up. A rout isn't final and may lead to even direr circumstances, but that's part of the fun and will make the end even more satisfying.

Like all the structural points, genre is irrelevant. The situation may look different across genres on the surface, but underneath it's the same; they have a win or a loss, but the main fight is yet to come.

The point is to ensure that things don't go according to plan and that you have another ace ready to play for your audience. Even if it looks like your protagonist has achieved everything they set out to do, you'll need to reveal the stakes are bigger than they thought.

Providing a false victory or false defeat should upend your audience's expectations, particularly as it comes when your protagonist is growing in confidence and starting to believe they can do more. It's part of the emotional roller coaster and ensures you don't get lazy as a story creator. If you merely meet your audience's assumptions on how things will play out, you're not entertaining them.

Following the false victory/defeat is a great time to throw in a quiet moment for reflection to give your protagonist a chance to reassess and deal with whatever issues they're facing so they have a chance to recover and refocus.

Whether you provide a false victory or false defeat (you can have both if you like), this structural point acts as a setback or realisation there's more to do, and it's going to be even more difficult than they first thought, perhaps impossible. It may represent a complete rout where any chances of success appear to be gone. The more you can convince your audience of this, the better.

Use it to your advantage to keep it interesting.

Put simply, the false victory/defeat is both a structural element and a strongly emotional part of your protagonist's journey. This is where they're likely to realise they've failed, there's no obvious way forward and the odds of success are insurmountable.

The more problems you can stack on them at this time, the better. A ticking clock works brilliantly.

Think of the false victory/defeat as that moment where, in something like a murder mystery, the detective has finally figured out who the murderer is and has all the evidence to bring them to justice, only to see their hard work dashed on the rocks of a technicality. They know who the killer is, but are powerless to stop them doing it again or to bring them to justice.

In something like a romance, the star-crossed lovers get torn apart, often with one of them falling into the arms of a rival or being cast out of whatever social situation they've been drawn into, making it near impossible to rescue their relationship.

The build up to the false victory/defeat misleads your protagonist into thinking they're close to whatever win they're after. Not having things go as planned is good (for your story, not your characters), and ideally should create a huge emotional impact for your audience.

How much fun is it (for you) when you lead your audience to believe the protagonist has won... only to have them discover everything's now far worse than it was before?

Examples

Castaway

Chuck is near death as he drifts. He even lacks the strength to stand and signal for help as a huge ship cruises past.

He's defeated.

Despite this, he still gets rescued, a victory, but the victory's not the war and the story's not over.

Ferris Bueller's Day Off

Cameron, after his mental funk wears off, comes to the realisation that the main problem is himself. It's a victory, but not the victory he needs.

Jeanie's lost the fight. Her mother arrives to pick her up from the police station, ensuring there's nothing she can do to catch Ferris out. It appears as if Ferris has got away with his day off.

Happy Death Day

Although Tree has discovered her murderer is a serial killer responsible for taking the lives of at least half a dozen other young women, the battle's not over.

What she doesn't know is that it's a false victory. The serial killer is a setup and the real killer is still at large.

Miss Congeniality

Gracie's won a small victory, the chance to stay and protect the contestants, but she's essentially lost the battle. She has to do it alone with no resources and no backup. She's even forced to hand in her badge and gun.

Monsters Vs Aliens

Susan, while being escorted to the incinerator by one of Gallaxhar's clones, gets saved by the other monsters. It's a false victory as the Earth is still about to be invaded and Susan no longer has her giant size and strength.

Pretty Woman

Vivian and Edward break up despite Edward's attempts to keep the relationship going, but his new offer is a relationship Vivian can no longer accept. It would keep her reliant on him, ensuring she can no longer determine her own fate. She accepts the defeat with grace and decides it's time for her to move on with her life. Unfortunately that doesn't include Edward.

Star Wars

Luke, Han and Chewie get away from the Death Star with the rescued Princess Leah, the droids and the battle station's plans. It's a victory, but a minor one. They might have gotten away with their freedom, but they're being tracked to the Rebel base. This is both a false victory (they escaped) and false defeat (being tracked).

The Matrix

Neo and Trinity have escaped with their lives, but everything else has gone wrong. It's a solid defeat. The only success was avoiding capture or death despite Cypher's betrayal.

Their reprieve from certain defeat is all they have left, and it's just a matter of time before even that will be taken from them when Morpheus breaks.

Twilight

Although Bella escapes town, it's a false victory. The threat James poses hasn't gone away, and there's still a good chance that Edward, herself, and possibly others will die before it's over.

Putting it into practice

To make this work, you need to set up the conditions for some kind of victory or defeat and upend those conditions in an unanticipated way.

If the conditions for victory are met, it's got to be made clear the conditions were an illusion and they've only won a battle, not the war. If they're not met, they need to understand that it's not a final defeat, and they've only lost the battle.

In either case, they just need to figure out another way to win.

- What are the conditions for a victory or defeat at this point of the story?
- How will meeting or failing against these conditions affect the remainder of the story?

23

REGROUP

By now your characters have had some sort of win or loss of the non-final variety. Perhaps they've barely escaped with their lives after things went wrong, been rejected in a relationship, or thought they'd come away with a clean win only to realise they've made things impossibly worse.

However they got here, this is the beginning of the end. Hopefully you've made things far direr than any of your characters could have anticipated earlier in the story.

It's time to face problems, lick wounds, bury wounded pride and come up with a whole new plan.

And that's essentially what this section of the story is all about. Your protagonist must take stock of their situation and come at it from another angle. Your audience needs to be fully behind them at this point too, desperately hoping everything will turn out okay (but unable to see how).

This is where you're going to give your characters, and consequently your audience, hope of some kind.

Whatever plan your protagonist decides on shouldn't make it obvious how things are going to turn out, but it has to be something they'll accept. Telegraph how it ends only if you're planning on upending it in a twist. Either way, no plan survives first contact with adversity, so you'll need to think of a few roadblocks and hurdles as they scramble to save it.

No matter what else happens, your protagonist and support cast need to proactively commit to a course of action. This is their last ditch effort, their final and only shot, and the consequences of failure have to be better than not trying at all.

So give them a plan and point them at the final battle, whether that battle's winning love, stopping the bad buy or preventing the end of the world.

It's time for your protagonist to 'suit up' and mount their final charge.

It's do or die - perhaps literally.

Examples

Cast Away

Chuck, safe now, arrives home, only to find that it's not what he was expecting. Everyone's moved on and he no longer feels as if he fits in. His experiences have changed him too much. He needs to take a new direction in life, but he's not sure what it is. Although his former fiancé is married with a child now, he still needs closure and decides to visit her. What he's facing is an inner struggle, and he needs a new plan. The plan is to take his old life back, but like most good plans, it's not likely to survive first contact with opposing forces. It will give him some sort of closure though.

Ferris Bueller's Day Off

As Jeanie's story was introduced first it must be concluded last. This means Cameron's story is almost complete. Cameron's regroup and return to normal plays out in its entirety before Jeanie's begin.

For Cameron, the victory appears to have been won. He's accepted the fact that he's been in a bad place and things need to change. The problem is that the Ferrari's odometer still shows over a hundred miles more than it should. The plan - jack up the car and reverse the engine so the odometer goes backwards.

Jeanie's been picked up by her mother from the police station and is on the way home, defeated in her quest to catch her brother out. That's when opportunity smiles. She gets a second chance to catch Ferris as he's running home after leaving Cameron's house. All she needs to do is get home before Ferris and expose him for the fraud he is.

Happy Death Day

Tree believes she knows who her murderer is now, and comes up with a whole new plan to turn the tables and end the loop. In an homage to Groundhog Day, she lives the 'perfect day' and becomes the person she wants to be. Afterward, she finally kills the serial killer, believing she's ended the cycle and freed herself from repeating the same day. It's another false victory, however. She wakes up once more in Carter's room with the day still on repeat.

The cupcake is the final clue in the puzzle.

Monsters Vs Aliens

Susan's still alive thanks to a rescue by her fellow monsters, but the invasion of Earth is underway now that Gallaxhar has the quantonium. Their new plan: destroy Gallaxhar's ship before the invasion can begin.

Pretty Woman

Vivian and Edward's time together is at an end and it's time for her to pack up and leave. She still wants the fairytale, but realises she'll never get it. She decides to take a new direction in life, leaving both her relationship with Edward and her life as a prostitute behind. Her new plan is to start over and take control of her life.

Star Wars

Thanks to Luke's escape from the Death Star with Princess Leia and R2D2, the Rebel Alliance is able to analyse the plans to the Death Star and find a small weakness. It's a tiny chance, but it's their only chance, and so the Rebel Alliance prepares for an assault on the Death Star. Luke suits up, piloting an X-wing fighter and joining the battle.

The Matrix

Neo's new plan is to save Morpheus, even if it costs him his life. Along with Trinity, they load up with weapons and prepare to re-enter The Matrix once more, this time to take on the Agents directly. It's a small hope and won't buy them victory, but saving Morpheus will ensure they aren't defeated either.

Twilight

After Bella, Alice and Jasper head away, James figures out the ruse and so the victory in getting Bella away safely is short lived. James now threatens Bella's mother, and so Bella makes her own plan – sacrifice herself in order to protect the people she loves. She needs to get to James, and comes up with a plan to escape her protectors and give herself up.

Putting it into Practice

- What new plan does your protagonist come up with?
- How do you plan to make this difficult?

24

INTO BATTLE

This is the moment your audience has been anticipating from the moment they started the story. Your protagonist's final battle plan is put into motion and everything is on the line. Your protagonist has suited up, prepped with intel, and is now charging into the fray. This is their final chance to achieve the outcome they're after.

If they fail here there'll be no second chance, and your audience should know it. Your audience needs to be just as invested as your characters, and totally unaware you've acted like an evil overlord and totally manipulated their emotions.

Everything that matters to your characters comes down to this part of the story.

Your audience should be invested in the outcome, uncertain about the outcome and tense with anticipation, just as your characters should be as they fight for everything they believe in.

All the meaning you can bring to it, the tension you build and the dire consequences of failure all amount to the impact you'll have on your audience.

This is where you show how you've taken your protagonist from unprepared to battle-ready, and demonstrate how they're applying everything they've learned for what they believe in.

Of course, you don't have to provide action in the form of physical combat. Plenty of stories aren't going to have a stand up fist-fight in a boxing ring where every punch matters, or show an epic battle of armies. The stakes could be decided in a battle of wits or a game of chess.

The final battle could be as simple as your protagonist finding enough courage to walk into a room and declare their love for someone, even if the only risk is humiliation.

No matter what it comes down to, if your characters don't have to struggle for anything at this point, why will an audience care if they get what they want – or fail?

They may not get what they're after, but they still need some sort of a win. Little Miss Sunshine demonstrates this beautifully when they lose the pageant but win the hearts of the audience.

Whatever your scenario and outcome, your characters need to be risking something and your audience must be backing them.

Examples

Cast Away

Chuck's home. He's caught up with friends and found he no longer fits in. The world is still the same, but he's different. The people around him take too much for granted; things he had to fight for on his island, like food and shelter, and now it's all being handed to him as if that were normal.

He goes into battle and visits his ex-fiancé, and they almost run away together. Almost. But running away with her won't give him the closure he needs.

He has to move on, not reignite the past.

The battle isn't about getting his old life back. It's about making a new life, and it's not until he sees his former fiancé that he realises this.

And so he leaves her for good this time, his only plan to deliver the final package he'd kept safe on the island, and from there to see where life takes him. It was never about getting home and getting the girl, it was about the freedom to determine his own fate.

He still doesn't know where he's going or what he's going to do, but he now knows he can't return to the life he had once lived. The battle was internal and he wins it.

Ferris Bueller's Day Off

Cameron's story: The Ferrari's odometer isn't going backwards, despite jacking the car up and putting it in reverse. Ferris offers to crack open the odometer and reverse it by hand, but Cameron chooses not to. At that point all his hurt and frustrations with his father bubble up and he takes out his anger on the car, knocking it off its jack. The Ferrari shoots out the back of the glass-walled garage and crashes. It's then that he realises the truth. The problem is his relationship with his father, not the car. It's time to sort that out. He's come to realise that now.

Jeanie's story: despite an epic sprint by Ferris, he fails to get home before Jeannie, but worse than that, Principal Rooney is there waiting for him. It's then that Jeannie opens the door, just in time to catch Ferris and witness him getting everything he deserves. She wins the battle, but it's a ploy. The battle was never with Ferris, and so she lets him off the hook.

Happy Death Day

After waking up yet again in Carter's room despite believing she'd ended the loop, Tree realises it's still not over. In a panic and determined to save herself, Tree returns to her room and packs to leave, getting away her only plan now. It's not until Lori lights the candle and offers Tree the cupcake again that Tree realises what happened. The night before Tree had eaten the cupcake, yet she'd died anyway. It means the serial killer was a red herring, as the only way Tree could have died was in her sleep – poisoned by the cupcake.

Her roommate Lori is the killer. In the final showdown, Tree takes on Lori and shoves her out the window to fall to her death.

Miss Congeniality

Gracie remains in the pageant, still determined to catch the killer, and thanks to her smarts and investigative work she figures out the plan - the bomb is in the crown and the winner will have her head blown off. Worse, her new best friend is the winner.

Gracie fights to prevent the plan causing an onstage uproar, and with the help of her partner who returns just in time, she saves the winner if not the show... or perhaps provides the best show ever.

Monsters Vs Aliens

Gallaxhar's ship is done for, but he's escaping with the quantoniam. With her monster friends trapped, it's up to Susan alone to stop him, but she's just a human now. The only way she can stop him is to become a monster again. She shoots the supports holding the quantoniam, and like the meteor which originally struck her, it falls onto her, imbuing her with its giant size and strength and giving her the power to stop Gallaxhar for good, which she does.

Pretty Woman

Vivian has chosen to leave Edward, but as she's preparing to leave, Edward's business partner, Phillip Stuckey, comes by Edward's hotel suite to talk things over with Edward. Edward's just altered the terms of a billion dollar deal thanks to Vivian's influence, and to Edward it feels good. To Philip Stuckey however, it's the worst outcome possible. He tries to take his anger out on Vivian, but Edward arrives and fights off Phillip.

Afterward, Edward tries once more to keep Vivian by his side, but it's still not the outcome wants. She wants the fairy tale, marriage to Edward, and so she takes control of her situation and leaves, free of both her relationship with Edward and her life as a prostitute. Of course, this is a romance, so even though the battle's over, the happy ending is yet to come. Edward, of course, caves and gives her the fairy tale.

Star Wars

The epic battle to destroy the Death Star amounts to an uneven contest of a few squads of X-wings taking on a moon-sized battle station. They're seriously outmatched, and they only have a tiny chance to exploit the Death Star's weakness.

The battle comes together in a single moment when Luke finally believes in himself, trusts his instincts and shoots the torpedoes into the heart of the Death Star, destroying it.

The Matrix

Neo fights Agent Smith alone, and although he prevails in the train station, Agent Smith returns and the chase is on. Neo needs to escape The Matrix or he'll be killed and the Nebuchadnezzar destroyed, but when he gets to the exit point he finds Agent Smith already there.

All the storylines come together at that point, and after Agent Smith shoots and kills Neo in The Matrix, Trinity's kiss revives him. It's what Neo needed. He wakes with insight and uses his newfound power to destroy Agent Smith and get back to the Nebuchadnezzar.

Twilight

Bella goes to James in order to save her mother, only to find it was all a trick. Her mother's not there. Fortunately, Edward and his vampire family catch up and they fight off James, killing him. The battle's not over though. Bella was bitten and will soon turn into a vampire unless Edward stops the process, which he does.

Putting it into practice

- What has your protagonist learned up to this point that will help them 'win the battle'?
- How exactly does your protagonist win?
- What is the cost of winning (if anything)?
- What does the antagonist lose?
- Why will this win satisfy your audience?

25

RETURN TO NORMAL

The purpose of this section is twofold. You want to:

- Illustrate how things are different for your protagonist compared with how they saw the world at the beginning of the story.
- Show internal changes in the protagonist - how they've grown (or outgrown who they used to be).
- This illustrates their character arc.

There are many ways of doing this.

In the Lord of the Rings, the hobbits quite literally return to the Shire and we see how their experience has changed them based on how they react to familiar surrounds.

Taking your characters to where they were at the beginning of the story makes it easier to demonstrate how they've grown, developed and changed from how they started out. They don't need to return to a place, though it's easier to demonstrate how they've changed if you do. They may no longer fit in, for instance, or finally fit in.

Showing them where they want to be rather than where they were will also do this, as will a character from their past who hasn't undergone their experience. Their lack of change will demonstrate the difference and show how much your protagonist has grown.

There are plenty of ways to show they're no longer the same person they were at the beginning. It could be as simple as walking away from everything they once thought was important.

It's the contrast that matters here. Demonstrate their growth in some way, whether that's the traditional 'go back to the village' scenario or some other illustration. Show your audience that your protagonist is a better person than they were at the beginning of the adventure. They need to have learned from their experience and the difference must have created some sort of positive change for themselves, the world, or both.

This will illustrate the protagonist's character arc as well as the theme.

Examples

Cast Away

In Cast Away, Chuck's been changed by his experience - his drive and business ambition have both collapsed under the weight of what happened to him, and now he finds himself at a crossroads with no direction in life. He's outgrown his old life, visiting with his fiancé has made that clear, but what does he do with his life now? He no longer fits in, and he's used to solitude and a much slower pace. How does he 'return to normal'?

The answer comes right after he's delivered the package he kept on the island with him. He literally stands at a crossroads where he's just spoken with a nice woman who appears to have been the person the package was for... and right there he finds a path back to a new normal. It's an internal adjustment, but it works for him. Although the movie finishes at that point, it's clear he's now got a direction. His life, which once belonged to the company he worked for, is now his own. The internal battle has been won and he's found his new normal.

Ferris Bueller's Day Off

Cameron's just trashed his father's car and Ferris offers to take the heat for it. But this is Cameron's story, and using his recently-learned maturity he takes responsibility for the situation. He decides to sit down with his father and have a chat rather than take the anticipated abuse. He's clearly a different person now, and you know everything's going to be much better for him.

Jeanie has won her own internal battle - she caught Ferris red-handed in front of Principal Rooney, everything she'd been aiming for that day. In a beautiful twist she demonstrates she's grown up and relinquishes her petty childishness, turning the tables on Principal Rooney. Rather than seeing Ferris get his comeuppance, she applies what she's learned from the kid in the police station and lets Ferris go. She then reveals to Principal Rooney that she has evidence he was the person in her house, a threat which could ruin him.

For both Cameron and Jeanie, their stories are over, but the movie isn't.

Ferris has one more trick to play - convince his parents the day off has done him good and he'll be fine for school tomorrow - which he does.

Happy Death Day

Tree has changed, and it's clear from the final scene just how much. She's back with Carter, a student she wouldn't have been seen in public with before. More to the point, she doesn't care who sees. She's a new person, a better person, and it shows.

Everything's back to normal, except that Tree has changed for the better.

Miss Congeniality

Although the pageant is over and the world is back to normal (the problem and the threat are gone), Gracie is clearly a different person. Although still devoted to her job and duties, she has gained a completely new appreciation for the contestants she once disdained. Thanks to her experience, she cares for them as friends rather than airheaded bimbos reliant on external praise of their physical form to feel valued. This new attitude comes out as she gives her speech as Miss Congeniality.

Monsters Vs Aliens

The world is safe once more, yet Susan is different. Not physically – she's still a giant, but she chose to be different in order to save the world, knowing there was no going back. This becomes even more apparent when her ex-fiancé Derek wants her back and she gives him the flick (literally).

She no longer needs him, and no longer values herself based on her relationship to him. She's her own woman now.

Pretty Woman

Vivian returns to her apartment, preparing to leave it for good. She's become a stronger and more confident woman, and the change is obvious. She's taken charge of her life, and that means turning down a great offer she would have been thrilled with at the beginning of the story.

Of course, this is a fairy tale, and she's Cinderella. To satisfy the audience she still needs to get the fairy tale ending, and she does. Edward turns up and offers her the life she wants, agreeing to marry her, but only because she's stood up for herself and took control of her future.

Star Wars

The Death Star's destroyed and so the threat it carried no longer exists. Luke's new normal is acceptance into the Rebel Alliance as a hero. It's everything he wanted, but he only got it because he believed in himself, something he hadn't been able to do at the beginning.

The medal ceremony at the end signifies this.

The Matrix

Agent Smith has been vanquished and Neo has become 'The One'. The Matrix still exists, but it's now a familiar place to Neo and carries little danger or menace for him. Where he never fit in before, he does now, and he's more than willing to use his new status to demonstrate this.

The Matrix remains the same. It's Neo who's different, and he's prepared to use that difference to make things better for everyone else in the Matrix.

Twilight

Having survived the threat from James, Bella is recovering in hospital. Her perception of the world is different now - in the beginning she knew nothing about vampires, but now she's dating one. Although she's still human, Bella understands the dangers of being involved with vampires, but she's comfortable with them. So long as Edward's with her, it's the life she wants.

Putting it into Practice

- How has your protagonist changed?
- How can you demonstrate how they've changed?

26

THEME REVISITED

Close to the end of your story, you need to revisit the theme in order to make your point about it. If you've read this book from start to finish you should be aware that somewhere near the beginning of your story the theme is stated in some way, usually in a conversation between the protagonist and another character who has some sort of influential relationship with them.

If possible, have the same character return at the end and clarify the theme and the point you're making.

For example, in a family drama your theme might be: 'Men make bad parents.' Your story would have debated both sides of this statement and come to a conclusion. At the end you get to revisit this concept, subtly pointing out whether or not men do make bad parents.

The keyword here is subtle. Point it out, but do so without being 'on the nose'. Don't tell them what they need to think. Illustrate it. In the case of 'men make bad parents', you could show it by having the father still be a bad parent at the end. If you disagree, show how he's become the father he needs to be.

The purpose of illustrating the theme is to make a statement about something. It's where the whole point of the story comes out – what you want to say about people, the world, or whatever you care about. This is why you wrote the story on an intellectual level. It's the deeper meaning.

A war between vampires and werewolves may be a metaphor for racism (and often is). What is it you want to say about racism? That no one is better off for it, perhaps? That everyone loses? How will your story illustrate that?

Whatever the theme and no matter how it's illustrated in your story, revisiting it is important for you, your characters and your audience. The main characters must show they've learned the truth of your theme, accepted it, and been changed by what they learn.

It's part of the characters' growth and what resonates with your audience on a deeper level. It's your theme that will keep them thinking about your story long after they've experienced it.

Your story may agree or disagree with any theme, or answer any question to your satisfaction, but it has to debate it fairly and come to a conclusion.

In this way, you're demonstrating what you believe in.

Can't stop thinking about it

What's the point of writing a story if it's forgotten the moment it's over? Getting people to keep thinking about your story long after they've finished it is the key to free marketing.

If people are thinking about your story, there's a chance they'll talk about it and become long-term fans.

Fans revisit stories they love, but more importantly, they tell their friends, write blog posts about them, buy copies as gifts, and even create their own fan fiction.

A genuine fan base also means free marketing for sequels, prequels, and other forms your story might take, such as games, apps, and translations.

Look at anything that's been popular over the last few decades and you'll see they all have a dedicated fan base that spreads the word organically.

The question is, how do you get this to happen? How do you create a massive fan base of people obsessed with your stories?

There's no guarantees, but two things help:

- Cater to your core audience.
- Make sure you have a strong theme that resonates well beyond your core audience.

Genre is specific. Theme is universal. Empathy and theme are what make people think about and discuss your story long after they've seen, read or heard it.

Examples

Cast Away

What has Chuck learned? Time's not the most important thing. It's what you do with your time that matters. What mattered to Chuck at the beginning of the story is vastly different to what matters to him at the end.

Ferris Bueller's Day Off

The theme of Ferris Bueller's Day Off is summarised in the conversation between Jeanie and the 'boy in the police station' played by Charlie Sheen. Jeanie is intensely angry with Ferris who she blames for her situation, because Ferris always seems to get away with everything when she can't. She tells this to the boy beside her, and he tells her that she's the problem, not Ferris. "Your problem is you," he states. He then elaborates: "You oughta spend a little more time dealing with yourself and a little less time worrying about what your brother does." Jeanie doesn't learn the lesson at that point, but in her final scene she demonstrates it by letting Ferris get away with his day's deceptions.

Similarly, just before Cameron trashes his father's car, he's lamenting about how he always takes abuse from his father. The day with Ferris has changed him however, because he now realises his relationship with his father isn't working. Referring to this, Cameron says, "Well he's not the problem. I'm the problem." In this statement he's expressing the story's theme once again, just as the boy at the police station had stated it to Jeannie. Cameron's realised he no longer has to take abuse - and never had to in the first place. He's learned the lesson, and he's a better person because of it. Things are going to change.

Finally, Ferris himself weighs in from his bed where he once again breaks the fourth wall and talks to the audience. "Life moves pretty fast. If you don't stop and look around once in a while, you could miss it." He's summing it all up. Live your own life and stop worrying about what everyone does or thinks of you.

Happy Death Day

There's a sticker on the back of Carter's dorm room door which says: *Today is the first day of the rest of your life*, which is thematic, but isn't the story's theme. Even so, it does reinforce part of the story's true theme. Theme should be subtle and reflected by changes in the protagonist's character. While Happy Death Day is largely designed to play with the tropes of the slasher genre, it contains a strong theme.

Like the song Cats in the Cradle, the theme is the same. "You reap what you sew." It's what Tree learns and why she changes. She doesn't want to be a superficial, selfish person who hurts other people. It's a lesson she learns and takes to heart, making her a better person in the end.

Miss Congeniality

Gracie went into the pageant with preconceived notions about what the pageant was about (exploitation), and found her expectations shattered as she came to care for the other contestants. She learned not to judge. The experience made her a better person, and in the end it transformed her. Her final speech demonstrates this.

Star Wars

What did Luke need to learn? He needed to learn to trust his feelings and believe in himself. He achieved that during the final battle against the Death Star, demonstrating it when he trusted himself to fire the torpedoes without the aid of a computer. Obi-Wan, talking to him as a ghost, gave him the final push he needed to realise this. You've got to believe in yourself if you want to accomplish anything.

The Matrix

Much like Luke Skywalker, Neo needed to believe in himself. At the beginning of the story he was rebelling without knowing why. In the end, he stands up for what he believes in, and it's that belief that gives him the insight he needs to succeed.

Twilight

What did Bella learn? She learns to fight for what she cares about, no matter the personal cost. It's what defines her relationship with Edward, and what allows her to win him in the end.

Putting it into practice

- What does your protagonist learn that's indicative of your story's theme?

27

THE PROMISE OF THE PREMISE

By now you should have a good understanding of how character and structure work together in what's often perceived as an unholy alliance: character and plot inseparably entwined like lovers.

Hopefully you've answered the questions peppered throughout. They're important and will give you a much stronger sense of your story and what it's going to take to make it work for your audience.

These questions should also provide a solid view of what you want that story will look like when complete.

No matter your process, you still need to do the hard stuff at some point. Write the story first if you must, but then go back and answer the questions in this book, and be honest with the story. If it's not working, sort it out before you go on a ten-year editing binge.

Breaking it down is important. The questions will push you toward ideas and answers you've probably never considered, making your story much stronger. It'll help you spot plot holes, find weaknesses, generate better ideas, and see it from a fresh perspective.

Figuring out your story before you write it, or at least exploring it from a technical perspective before launching into the editing process, will save you a lot of time later on.

What are you promising your audience?

At some point you need to be able to explain exactly what your story's about – to state it clearly and concisely. This is your story's premise, but it's also your promise to your audience.

Your audience includes the gatekeepers of industry (agents, managers, producers, publishers, directors – whoever can take your story and do more with it than you can alone). Your entire audience (including the gatekeepers) expect clarity, both in the writing and the overarching story premise.

It's now time to create a promise in a very simple (but difficult to produce) premise.

What you're promising is a story geared toward your specific audience, something you think they'll love.

Explaining what you're promising is often difficult because you're trying to distil an entire story into a couple of dozen words at most, but if you can't explain your story in ten seconds you probably don't know it well enough. Any attempt to explain or write it at that point will reflect the muddle of your thoughts and make it a difficult sell.

If you can't see yourself writing an intriguing premise in twenty five words or less, here's a simple process to follow that'll help.

First, answer the questions in the book. That'll help give you clarity overall and help you go from big to small.

Next, your story has a heart. The questions up to this point will have helped you see that picture. Now it's time to get into it.

Begin by thinking in broad strokes, not detail:

- Who's your protagonist?
- What's their overarching problem?

- Why does your protagonist care about the problem?
- What's the story's tone and genre?

Broad strokes. Big concepts. This is not a place to get bogged down in the detail.

What's the overall story from beginning to end? Once you've given that a little thought, try this formula. In twenty five words or less, explain:

- who it's about
- what they want (stop the threat)
- who or what's standing in their way
- the hook (find some irony in the situation if possible).

Additionally, you need to show genre and tone within your statement.

Answer each bullet point separately, and then combine them to create a single sentence of up to twenty-five words that broadly explains your story and lets your audience know what you're promising. For example:

- It's about a human woman.
- She wants to survive.
- A cyborg is trying to kill her
- She's being hunted because of a child she's yet to conceive.

Put together: *"A woman is being hunted by a cyborg from the future because of a child she's yet to conceive." Terminator.*

Specific, yet only nineteen words. It also gives a pretty solid impression of the genre and the ideal audience.

So how do you go about doing this for your own story?

Break it into four parts:

- **Who is your story about?** *Don't name them.* Describe them. It could be a retired pirate, a corrupt cop, a mad inventor – be general, but clear and descriptive.
- **What do they want?** A retired pirate might want to get back into the game. A mad inventor might hope to go back in time and change the past. A soldier might want to survive a war to see their family once more.
- **What's standing in their way?** Internal or external? A physical threat? Their own conscience or fears?
- **Show the hook.** What makes it stand out and demand attention? Irony works really well here, but it's also the hardest thing to find.

Those parts don't necessarily have to be in order when you write your premise, but they do have to be there in some way.

If you do this for each story you write, you'll have the basis for a strong, focused and tight story. A tight premise also looks great at the top of any pitch you send.

As a bonus, if someone asks you what your story's about, you can tell them in twenty-five words or less (if you take much longer to pitch your story, you probably don't know what it's about).

What's your premise? Give it a go and test it on friends, family, or even random strangers while you're waiting in line to see a movie. If you get interest, there's a good chance you're onto a winner.

28

RULES FOR YOUR STORY WORLD

Story rules? Seriously?

Who wants rules? They're limitations, right?

Well, err, yes. That's the point. Without rules you can do whatever you want. It's like picking up a guitar without ever having played one and strumming out random off-key twangs and calling it music.

Rules are what you're promising your audience about your story. Rules set boundaries, create a framework, and make life far more interesting (difficult) for your characters.

- Humans can't breathe underwater? That's going to make it challenging to cross the ocean.
- Can't wave your hand to fix a broken limb? Surviving in the wilderness could be tricky after an injury like that.
- Can't ignore the known laws of physics, chemistry and biology? Space exploration's not going to be simple.

If you don't like applying story limitations, think of rules as conflict generation software designed to make your story more interesting.

Yes, they might force you to think a little more and work a bit harder, but that's what makes a story interesting.

As with pregnancy and nuclear warfare, story rules matter to the characters involved, and your characters are always involved. Your audience won't appreciate it if you tell them your protagonist's pregnant and two scenes later the baby jumps bodies and it's her best friend who's pregnant instead.

Whatever you tell your audience about your story is a rule. If you say someone's pregnant, the consequences need to be considered.

Take the Road Runner cartoon, for example. Do an internet search on 'Road Runner rules' and you'll pull up dozens of sources showcasing Chuck Jones' rules for the iconic cartoon. They're brilliant.

They succinctly encapsulate the story universe in which the Road Runner cartoon takes place, define the relationship between the Road Runner and the Coyote, and generate innate conflict. If you're too busy to look them up, here they are:

1. The Road Runner cannot harm the Coyote except by going "Beep, beep!"
2. No outside force can harm the Coyote – only his own ineptitude or the failure of ACME products.
3. The Coyote could stop anytime – if he were not a fanatic.
4. No dialogue ever, except "Beep, beep".
5. The Road Runner must stay on the road – otherwise, logically, he would not be called Road Runner.
6. All action must be confined to the natural environment of the two characters – the southwest American desert.
7. All materials, tools, weapons, or mechanical conveniences must be obtained from the ACME Corporation.
8. Whenever possible, make gravity the Coyote's greatest enemy.

9. The Coyote is always more humiliated than harmed by his failures.

I particularly love rules 8 and 9 which set the tone for the show, as well as number 3, which is where most of the conflict comes from. The overall value of the nine rules defines universal story considerations:

- They set boundaries.
- Boundaries are important because they create your story's landscape. What's the point of calling a story a space opera if all the action's confined to a holiday resort by a beach in Fiji?
- They define the nature of the story's conflict.
- The nature of a story's conflict sets the story's tone. It can be funny as it's intended to be in the Road Runner, or it can deal with issues as heavy as domestic violence, abuse and bullying.
- They determine the relationships between characters. Relationships carry and define the emotional context.
- They are the underlying causes of a story's conflict and the consequences your characters must deal with.

While you don't want to go overboard with rules, creating a handful of basic rules guides story creation and its inherent conflicts, no matter the setting.

For example, in the X-Files TV series, one of the rules is that Scully and Mulder never get together romantically. That rule got bent occasionally, but overall it dictated how the two main characters worked together. Their relationship remained professional, not romantic, which created plenty of sexual tension.

Similarly, if you create a system of magic for a fantasy world, your rules will help you define the nature of its magic, the conditions of its use, and limit what it can do. If a wizard can click their fingers and solve all their problems, your story's going to be resolved in the opening sentence. But, if magic's limitations cause problems you'll have a good story.

Rules might make it difficult for you as the writer, but they make a story far more interesting for an audience.

In a show like Buffy the Vampire Slayer, the rules look something like this:

- Slayers are girls. Always.
- When a slayer dies, another rises in her place.
- You can kill a vampire with a wooden stake through the heart, with fire, or by beheading it.
- The Hellmouth spawns and attracts all sorts of demonic creatures, not just vampires.
- Magic always comes with a cost.
- Wherever possible, mix comedy with horror.

If you're a fan of the show you could probably add a few more. The point is, you want to keep your story rules broad yet simple. Use them to introduce inherent conflict. Avoid bending or breaking them without a strong story justification.

Fun game:

- Pick a show, a movie or a book you're familiar with.
- Try and figure out its basic rules.

How many rules do you need?

Keep your rules to ten or less. The more you have, the more difficult it'll be to keep track of them. That's a rabbit hole you want to avoid twisting your creative ankle in.

Asimov created just three rules for his robot science fiction stories.

They're commonly known as Three Laws of Robotics and were introduced in his 1942 short story 'Runaround'.

They are:

- A robot may not injure a human being or, through inaction, allow a human being to come to harm.
- A robot must obey orders given it by human beings except where such orders would conflict with the First Law.
- A robot must protect its own existence as long as such protection does not conflict with the First or Second Law.

These three rules set the scene and tone, define genre, and drive the plot for many of his robotics stories. As you can see, when it comes to overarching story rules, less is more. You really only need a handful.

In James Cameron's movie Avatar, one of the rules was that the operator of an avatar must be genetically compatible with the avatar. This particular rule drove a large portion of the story's plot and forced an unlikely character into the lead role, creating all kinds of conflict.

Like Asimov's robot rules and the rules for Buffy the Vampire Slayer and Roadrunner, a single set of rules may apply to any number of stories you create. This makes them good for developing broader story worlds which can be used across extended storylines and multiple mediums.

Rules make your story unique

By combining several rules you get unique story drivers.

If you don't have something specific in mind such as Asimov's Three Laws of Robotics, think more generically, such as:

- All action must take place in a specific area or place (like a café, hospital, spaceship or microcosm).

- A known 'rule' of physics can be broken in certain circumstances.
- Magic can only be summoned by stripy-eared pink-eyed floating elephants with grudges against humanity (okay, that's not generic, but hopefully it got your attention).

Create rules to specifically affect your characters (or more to the point, your protagonist), such as the expensive avatar that can only be operated by a genetically compatible person. For example:

- A particular hospital treats patience as products instead of people.
- Magic fails under certain conditions.
- Specific relationships are forbidden.

What happens when you introduce a character into one of those places and situations, and the story rule causes conflict? In short, you get a unique story driver which sets your story apart.

No rules mean no problems. No problems mean no conflict. No conflict means no story.

Consider your audience

Rules give your audience a reference point for consistency and story interpretation, as well as an intellectual challenge when you throw problems at your characters which aren't easily solved.

As the writer, rules challenge you and make your story far more interesting to write. Your protagonist's space ship can't break the speed of light? Great! So how do they cross galaxies when they need to? Your audience wants to know as well.

Have fun bending your rules, but don't break them within the context of your story. No kid wants to see the Coyote get genuinely hurt or the Roadrunner caught and eaten.

Putting it together

Develop three to ten rules for your story universe which:

- set boundaries
- influence the relationships between characters
- create problems which contribute to the underlying causes of your story's conflict.

29

TROUBLESHOOTING

Cause and effect

If your story's not working, write a cause and effect statement. There's a good chance your problem rests there.

What's a cause and effect statement? It goes like this:

- Cause = Effect.
- Effect = New Cause.
- New Cause = New Effect.

To write it out in slightly more story-like terms:

- Because someone does A, the consequences mean B happens.
- Because B happens, this causes C...
- Because of C... and repeat."

The cause and effect can be anything, but anything isn't necessarily the best way to go about it. What you're looking for is significant story beats that cause a chain of events from beginning to end.

Break the chain and you break the story.

Writing a cause and effect statement will help you identify flow and consequence. The concept is quite simple, but the results are extremely powerful.

In its simplest terms, it means that if something happens, it needs consequences. If there are no consequences, why is it in your story?

Additionally, those consequences must affect the rest of the story, one building on the last. What's the point of an alien invasion if nothing really changes, or two people falling in love if they don't have to fight for it?

If something happens and has no flow-on effect, there's an issue with your story. You can probably remove the event without consequence.

Start with the big story points - one statement and consequence per story quarter, for instance. For example:

Setup

- Bella moves to Forks - (and the consequence is) she meets Edward.

Adventure Begins

- Edward saves Bella's life - (and the consequence is) Bella discovers Edward's a vampire.

Things Get Serious

- Bella and Edward hook up - (and the consequence is) Bella becomes involved in the 'vampire world', putting her in conflict with James.

Ending

- James tries to kill Bella - (and the consequence is) Edward and his family destroy James and save Bella.

The above example provides a very broad cause and effect overview in relation to the main story arc, but you can break it down much further, either by plotline or character arc.

Fun exercise

- Pick your favourite story and identify the four main causes/effects that carry the story from beginning to end.
- Once you've done the basic cause and effect, break it down into more detail – three cause/effects for each part of the story.

These cause/effect statements can run into a lot of pages when you get down to detailing single storylines.

The point is to demonstrate an unbroken chain of events and consequences from the beginning of the story to the end, each reliant on the last.

In the next example, Star Wars is broken down into three sequences per part. It includes each major cause and effect for each part of the story:

Setup

- **Cause:** Leah has the stolen plans for the Death Star
- **Effect:** Her Rebel ship is being pursued by the Empire
- Leah saves the intel by jettisoning the plans in the droid R2D2
- R2Dd has orders to find Obi-Wan Kenobi
- After landing on Tatooine, R2D2 gets captured by Jawas
- R2D2 gets sold to Luke Skywalker

Adventure Begins

- R2D2 runs away
- R2D2 consequently leads Luke to Obi-Wan Kenobi
- Luke survives the attack on the farm (because he's not there)
- They go to Mos Eisley
- Luke & Obi-Wan Kenobi are discovered by the Empire's troops
- They escape aboard the Millennium Falcon

Things Get Serious

- The captured Leah refuses to reveal information (follows on from the opening scenes and her capture)
- The Death Star is used to destroy Leah's home world of Dantooine
- The Millennium Falcon is caught by the Death Star when it turns up at Dantooine
- Luke and Obi-Wan avoid capture and sneak from the Millennium Falcon onto the Death Star
- Luke rescues Leah and escapes the Death Star with the stolen plans (Luke and Leah's storylines converge)
- They're being tracked by the Empire as they flee to the Rebel base

Ending

- The plans get analysed at the Rebel base
- The plans reveal a tiny weakness in the Death Star
- The Death Star approaches the Rebel base, intent on destroying the Rebel Alliance
- Rebels launch a desperate counter-attack
- Luke, part of the counter-attack, destroys the Death Star
- Celebratory high fives, hugs, and an awards night

If you look at the story progression, each event leads to the next, creating an unbroken chain of causes and effects showing two separate (but converging) storylines.

For something like this, you could just do Luke or Leah's storylines. Or Han Solo's.

Even then, this is still a broad overview which ignores more than a few characters and events, such as the antagonist's part.

In your own story, try separating out each character's storyline (particularly if one of them isn't working), writing a cause and effect statement for each main character (even breaking them down into scenes, for instance). If you want to give it a secondary use, try recompiling the character-based cause and effect statements together to outline the overall story.

The Star Wars example above is only broken down into simple, broad plot points. Adding in emotional story arcs will give your stories much more depth. For example, in Star Wars, Obi-Wan dies. This has emotional impact for Luke, and he's justifiably upset as Obi-Wan was his mentor and last connection to his life on Tatooine. This is shown in Luke's immediate reaction to the death, but also in a later scene when Luke's feeling depressed. Cause and effect.

It's up to you how much detail you need before writing your story, but the more you can figure out beforehand the easier it is to spot problems before they become issues.

If you can't see the consequences of a scene either immediately or later in the story, then there's a story problem. Deal with it before you move on. A scene that leads to nothing usually has no place in a story.

30

BUILDING YOUR STORY BIBLE

A story bible is an industry-standard term for a document or other form of repository where you collate everything important about your story for easy reference. Your 'one source of truth'.

Change the name if you like. It might be your Tome of Story Insight or a simply your Story Wiki.

It's just a name, after all. This is for you, not the industry.

Keeping it together

There's a lot of questions in this book, and they're hard. Tackle them one at a time if necessary. One a day will get you there eventually.

As you create answers, put them in your story bible.

Very shortly you'll have have a detailed concept of your story.

Questions about you

These questions are about what you want to say. They are the most fundamental issues to deal with before tackling your story.

A story's 'cool factor' is all well and good, but it's pointless if it doesn't mean anything to anyone.

Only you can give your story meaning, and that means finding a way to care about it. What wrongs do you want to point out about the world, its people, or how we treat each other? What internal battles are you fighting?

The Care Factor

- *How do you feel about your story?*
- What excites you about it?
- Why do you want to tell it?
- Why do you care?
- *What are you trying to make other people feel?*
- When someone finishes your story, do you want to see tears or inspiration on their face? Something else?
- *How are you going to engage your audience's emotions?*
- What issues are you going to address that will affect their feelings?
- How are you going to make your audience care about your characters and what happens to them?

Tip: the more your characters care, the more your audience will care.

Theme

- Write down at least one topic you care about.
- Turn it into a statement or question you can explore or argue demonstrable by your story. I.e. 'Slavery is wrong!'

Rules

Every story needs rules. Create and write down as many as ten story/world building rules which:

- set boundaries
- influence the relationships between characters
- contribute to the underlying causes of your story's conflict.

Overarching story issues

Write down what you need to know about your story before you can write or revise it.

- What is your story's main problem?
- What is worth fighting for (resources, ideals, power, etc?)
- What are the consequences for your story world if your protagonist fails to resolve the main story problem?
- How you will resolve the story problem
- What cool stuff happens? Think promo/trailer moments.

About your protagonist

You need to know who your protagonist is and what they're fighting for. Clarify it by writing answers to the following questions:

- What consequences will your protagonist face if they fail to resolve the main story problem?
- Why do they care about the consequences (why is it personal)?
- What does your protagonist need to do to satisfactorily resolve the problem?
- What do they want? This is external, like saving their friend or ending tyranny.
- What do they need? This is internal, like courage or belief.

About your antagonist

Everyone loves a well-developed antagonist. What differentiates them from a protagonist isn't their 'evil' ways, it's the fact that when presented with a moral choice, they always make the wrong choice. That makes them interesting.

- What does your antagonist need to do to satisfactorily resolve the story problem for themselves?
- What will be the results if your antagonist succeeds? Write answers for: your antagonist and the larger story world.
- What if they fail?

About your other characters

A support cast will generally enrich your story and ensure events can be seen from other points of view. This can be demonstrated in anything from dialogue and action, to actual scenes delivered from their perspective.

What are the consequences for each of your other main characters if the main story problem isn't resolved to their satisfaction? Write answers for your:

- Protagonist
- Antagonist
- Others

Structural questions

First half

- What questions will your story raise in the first half?
- Ie, who's behind the plot to kill the [important person]?
- What holds your protagonist back in the first half?

Second half

- How will your story answer the questions raised in the first half?

- Why does your protagonist become proactive in the second half?
- What does your protagonist learn in the beginning that will help them in the end?
- How (specifically) do they apply what they've learned in order to win at the end?

Introduction (first quarter)

- Who are your main characters (in order of appearance)?
- How will you introduce them in the context of the story?
- How will you let your audience know what's unique or special about your story world?
- How will you introduce your story's main problem?

Middle (second and third quarters)

The middle educates your protagonist and equips them to fight the last battle.

- What specific lessons will you use to educate your protagonist (and other characters)?
- How will you demonstrate these lessons in the context of the story?

Ending

- How will your protagonist use what they've learned?

The inciting incident

Something a little out of the ordinary heralds change.

- What are you going to introduce, remove, or foreshadow in your story world during the inciting incident?
- How does the inciting incident affect the story?

- How does your protagonist act or react?
- Write down an idea for a scene that will demonstrate the inciting incident.

Call to adventure

This is where your protagonist is given an option to agree to participate in your story.

- Which character calls your protagonist to adventure?
- What are the consequences of saying no?
- What are the consequences of saying yes?
- Write down an idea for a scene that will demonstrate the call to adventure.
- What characters are involved?

Fateful decision

Your protagonist makes a decision on how to proceed. The more difficult the choice, the better.

- What decision does your protagonist make in order to define their adventure?
- What are the costs of their decision?
- What are the potential rewards?
- What decision would your ideal audience member make in the same circumstances?

Thrust into new world

Your protagonist is now outside their comfort zone.

- What has changed for your protagonist?
- How do they deal with it?

Explores new world

This is where the fun happens. Make it fun.

- What are you going to reveal to your protagonist about their story world?
- How will you reveal it?
- How will it benefit the protagonist?
- What is your protagonist going to learn about themselves or the world?
- How are they going to feel about it?
- Why are these things important to your story?

Midpoint

If you can, throw in a twist or surprise that turns your story sideways at this point.

- What change demonstrates things are getting more serious?
- What is the first thing your protagonist does to demonstrate they're getting more proactive?

All is lost

Everything goes sideways and it's quite likely a major support character is killed or sidelined.

- What plans, hopes or dreams did your protagonist expect to realise?
- How are those plans, hopes or dreams destroyed at the all is lost moment?

The darkest hour

The emotional fallout from the all is lost moment.

- What event or realisation triggers the darkest hour for your protagonist?

- What are the emotional consequences for your protagonist?

False victory/defeat

A win or loss at this point isn't final, and often causes an escalation in problems.

- What are the conditions for a victory or defeat at this point of the story?
- How will meeting or failing against these conditions affect the remainder of the story?

Regroup

Your protagonist (and support crew) come up with a new plan to solve the story problem.

- What new plan does your protagonist come up with?
- How do you plan to make this difficult?

Into battle

Your protagonist (and support crew) implements the new plan to deal with the story's main problem, usually risking everything.

- What are they risking if they fail?
- What has your protagonist learned up to this point that will help them 'win the battle'?
- How exactly does your protagonist win?
- What is the cost of winning (if anything)?
- What does the antagonist lose?
- Why will this win satisfy your audience?

Return to normal

Like the beginning, but in reverse, along with the consequences of what's happened.

- How has your protagonist changed?
- How can you demonstrate how they've changed?

Theme revisited

- What has your protagonist learned that's indicative of your story's theme?

31

PUTTING IT TOGETHER

Now you know a lot more about your story and why you're writing it, it's time to put it together in a more meaningful way. As the word 'outline' is often viewed as a fetid cesspool of twisted hatreds, we'll refer to it as your yellow brick road to the fabled land of epic beauty.

First of all, write down the title of the story if you have one. If not, try something descriptive such as the protagonist's name or what the story's about. For instance:

Sword and Sorcery and Spaceships
(working title)

Like everything in this yellow brick road to the land of epic storytelling, it's adjustable, fixable or delete-able. Consider it a working document.

Next, grab your premise and write it below the title.

Premise: *A farm boy learns space magic while on a mission to shatter the Evil Overlord's Disco Ball.*

Now if that's as far as you want to take it, no problems... you can sort out the remaining details as you write, and then spend a lot of time rewriting and editing. I'd suggest a few more steps on your yellow brick road. Write down the names of the protagonist, the antagonist, and at least one other person the protagonist can shoot the breeze with, confide in, or learn something from. Also, include the names of any other major characters you know about at this point.

Now, for each of those characters, do the premise exercise. Everyone's a hero in their own lunchtime, after all, and this helps you get to know them and give them a solid part in your story.

For Sword and Sorcery and Spaceships, your main characters might be: Farm Boy, Magic Swordsman, Lord Shine The Misunderstood, Tinny the Loyal Slave, Princess Sharpshooter and Captain McConMan. Maybe DropBear and Metal Mouth if you're feeling generous.

Once you write a story premise for each you'll have half a dozen story arcs running through your story. Some will be far more important than others, but it'll add variety and conflict.

Write down the following.

Opening scene:

Theme Expressed:

Inciting Incident:

Call to Adventure:

Fateful Decision:

Thrust into New World:

Explores New World:

All is Lost:

Darkest Hour:

False Victory/Defeat:

Regroup:

Into Battle:

Return to Normal:

Theme Revisited:

Closing Scene:

Now, write down what happens at each of those major structural points.

Underneath each point, in bullet form, write down the names of each character who'll be present (and why if you can).

For Example

Opening scene: Spaceship battle over a desert planet.

- Lord Shine The Misunderstood - chasing Princess Sharpshooter who has stolen his favourite Playlist.
- Princess Sharpshooter - wants to share the Playlist with the rest of the world.

Theme Expressed: Farm Boy laments he doesn't have enough belief in himself to take a risk and join the Disco war.

- Farm Boy - Wants to be somewhere else.

Inciting Incident: Tinny the Loyal Slave runs away to share Disco Playlist with the Magic Swordsman.

- Farm Boy - Chasing Tinny the Loyal Slave
- Tinny the Loyal Slave - On a quest to find the mythical Magic Swordsman
- Metal Mouth - Comic Relief

Call to Adventure: While pursuing his runaway slave, Farm Boy meets the Magic Swordsman, who offers him an awesome space adventure.

- Farm Boy - No Can Do. Gotta go home before I'm grounded.
- Magic Swordsman - Seeking a new apprentice
- Tinny the Loyal Slave - Plans Delivered
- Metal Mouth - Comic Relief

Fateful Decision: Farm Boy accepts the call after Lord Shine The Misunderstood's White Knights demonstrate accurate shooting skills for the only time ever.

- Farm Boy - Home's Toast. What's in Space?
- Magic Swordsman - Hold my hand and I'll show you the path to enlightenment
- Tinny the Loyal Slave - Courier Duties
- Metal Mouth - Comic Relief

Thrust into New World: Check out the new city in the valley below!

- Farm Boy - Wow! So that's a city?
- Magic Swordsman - Yup. Bit of a cesspool if you ask me
- Tinny the Loyal Slave - Veep Veep
- Metal Mouth - What about me? I'm here too.

Explores New World: Farm Boy goes for a drink and sees Magic Swordsman in action.

- Farm Boy - Cool! Drinks All Around!
- Magic Swordsman - I'm not paying!
- Captain McConMan - I like blasters.

All is Lost: Farm Boy gets gobbled up by TrashPack.

- Captain McConMan - I can blast radios.

- Princess Sharpshooter - Hey guys, check out this cool waterslide!
- Farm Boy - Me next!
- DropBear - Holds nose.

Darkest Hour: Magic Swordsman becomes the Magic Ghost.

- Magic Swordsman - Hit me if you... Doh!
- Lord Shine The Misunderstood - Yet I hit nothing but air? Weird.
- Farm Boy - Nooooooo!!!!!
- Princess Sharpshooter - Time to disco boys!
- Captain McConMan - Blasters are better than swords, see?
- Tinny the Loyal Slave - Clearing out
- DropBear - Shooting better than a White Knight.
- Metal Mouth - Comic Relief

False Victory/Defeat: Farm Boy escapes Lord Shine The Misunderstood's trap.

- Farm Boy - So, this is like a big blaster with a chair, right? And I shoot the White Knights with it?
- Princess Sharpshooter - I want a turn!
- Captain McConMan - Shuddup kid and shoot!
- Tinny the Loyal Slave - back to courier duties
- DropBear - Woohoo! I can fly!
- Metal Mouth - Comic Relief.

Regroup: Oh look, the playlist puts a hole in Lord Shine The Misunderstood's Disco Ball that goes all the way to its core. How convenient. If only we could get close enough to do it.

- Farm Boy - Pick me! Pick me!
- Princess Sharpshooter - Yep Brother, you can do that.
- Captain McConMan - Pfft.

Into Battle: Farm Boy and a bunch of orange-shirts mount X-branded Space Horses and hit the oversized Disco Ball with Lord Shine The Misunderstood's playlist.

- Farm Boy - Woohoo. I can ride Spaces Horses with ZERO lessons! I'm turning up the music!
- Tinny the Loyal Slave - Someone shot me? But... no fair!

Return to Normal: High Fives! Confetti. Sibling hugs. Party time in the Space Horse stable.

- All the Good Guys except Magic Ghost - We won! How unexpected.

Theme Revisited: Farm Boy accepts Bravery Award from Princess Sharpshooter, acknowledging his newly-acquired belief in his risk-taking skills.

- All the Good Guys except Magic Ghost - We scrub up good for a party, don't we?

Closing Scene: Almost all the good guys are still alive and happy about it.

Fill in the blanks

Now join the main structural points utilising a generous helping of logical scenes. Use hints to indicate the importance or function of each scene by adding creative leaders such as Ticking Clock, Emotional High, Emotional Low, Cliffhanger, Twist, Epic Reveal, Rising Tension and whatever else you can think of.

It doesn't have to be spectacularly detailed, but the more you put in now the easier the writing will be and the less rewriting and editing you'll have to do later on.

32

AND THAT'S A WRAP

By now you should know that creating a successful story means you have to make people feel what you want them to feel.

I've shown you what works most of the time for most of the people, but if there's a secret to storytelling you'll find it's different for every story and every person.

Sometimes writers strike it lucky and a story resonates with their audience, but many such writers find themselves unable to repeat a success because they don't know what they did right, and consequently their success is fleeting. They're not students of story. They're not professional storytellers. They're not like you.

It doesn't matter how clear and concise you are, how technically proficient you become, or how wild and fanciful your ideas are unless you can get people to care for your characters and what happens to them.

What is it you're angry about or hopeful for? What topics matter to you? Why should your story matter to anyone *but* you?

No audience (pets, plants, divinities and inanimate objects aside) means no one will ever experience your story, and if they don't then what you want to say isn't going to be heard.

Isn't your story a little more valuable than that?

Our brains are hard-wired to hear stories, but we're not hard-wired to tell them. Storytelling is a skill that needs to be mastered, and mastery takes effort. Fortunately you get better at it with practice and life experience.

So live life and read stories. Get interested in people and events, discoveries and history, and anything else that takes your fancy. Experience as much as you can and never let your mind grow old (even if your body has no choice). The richer you can make your stories, the better.

Consume stories with an eye to understanding them. Break them down and go over them repeatedly. It's how we learn.

Most of all, figure out who you want to tell your stories to and why those stories will be important to them, and write for those people. A broader audience may enjoy them too, but you've got to commit to your core audience first.

You're a storyteller, so tell stories in whatever form you wish, and touch as many hearts and minds as you can.

You've started on that path, but this is just the beginning.

Now go write.

TAKE THE NEXT STEP

FOR SCRIPTWRITERS AND NOVELISTS ALIKE

Take the next step

Grab the workbook that's right for you

PLEASE LEAVE A REVIEW

Thank you for reading *Character and Structure: An Unholy Alliance*. I hope you got as much out of reading it as I got from writing it.

If you found it useful and have the time, please leave a brief review on Amazon, Goodreads, or wherever you buy good books.

Reviews are the best way to spread the word about stories you like, and for many authors, the only way.

ABOUT THE AUTHOR

Chris Andrews is an author of science fiction, fantasy and horror.

Website - http://chrisandrews.me

Stay in Touch
Subscribe to Chris's Newsletter

ALSO BY CHRIS ANDREWS

Novels

Divine Prey - Normagaell Saga I - A Veil of Gods Novel

Short Stories

Any Job in a Haze - A Veil of Gods Short Story

Promises Promises - A Veil of Gods Short Story

Silver Rain on a Moonlit Night - A Veil of Gods Short Story

Wyvern's Blood - A Veil of Gods Short Story

Merrie Dawn - A Science Fiction Short Story

Books on Writing

Character and Structure: An Unholy Alliance

Printed in Great Britain
by Amazon

53451367R00113